BEYOND SURVIVING:

FROM RELIGIOUS OPPRESSION TO QUEER ACTIVISM

JOSHUA MOON JOHNSON, ED.D.

ISBN: 978-1508518860

Printed in partnership with
Purple Distinctions Self Publishing
www.purpledistinctions.com

Printed in the United States of America

DEDICATION

I dedicate this book to the brave students who

selflessly shared their stories in order to

give others a better experience.

Your resilience, passion, and courage inspire me.

FOREWORD

Rarely does a book come along that speaks with such candor and honestly about a timely and important topic as *Beyond Surviving: From Religious Oppression to Queer Activism*. The title speaks volumes to the need to help our children and students understand themselves and to educate our families, communities, and religious organizations about the opportunities on how to practice love. In my professional career, I have read and been apart of many conversations that addressed LGBTQ issues; however, Dr. Johnson has laid out his work through the voices of the students with such a powerful force.

If one is a sincere person and has the true love that Jesus Christ left us with, one will wonder how anyone can treat another in such a harsh way. In fact, I ponder what individuals are preaching in churches if not the following verse. Matthew 22:37–39 "Jesus said to him, 'You shall love the LORD your God with all your heart, with all your soul, and with all your mind.' This is the first and great commandment. And the second is like it: 'You shall love your neighbor as yourself.'"

In fact, the stories of students in *Beyond Surviving* show a great deal about the social conditions of our families and communities. The students' stories show us that what we could use so much more of in our society is to understand and to love. The stories also reveal the amount of hatred that one must face to live a life of honesty and authenticity. It is unfortunate that many of these students were raised in what many would call "Christian homes." It is unfortunate that many of the students faced such turmoil in trying to reconcile the disequilibrium of their faith, love for Christ, sexual identity, and place in this world in such harsh ways. It is no wonder why many of the students in this book and LGBTQ individuals end up abandoning their religion, faith, and Christ. It is sad to me that Churches and families are not the safe places where individuals can be loved and be shown compassion.

Perhaps this book will be a call to arms for many. Perhaps it will be the one book to make parents sob with understanding about how difficult it is to live a life of honestly by just being oneself. Perhaps, it will also inspire churches to rise to the call to practice the kind of love that Jesus showed the harlot at the well. More importantly, this book will give individuals the courage to build a life that matters. To live a life where couples might have the support of their families, churches, and communities. To live a life in a society might offer them simple love and support. This book does not speak only to the difficulty that LGBTQ individuals have to overcome to just survive; it also projects loudly the importance of keeping a vision and dream for your life.

Dr. Johnson has taken a bold step in being a literary activist to make a difference in the lives of LGBTQ individuals. He knows first-hand the reality of living in a world where the good, the bad and the ugly walk hand in hand. I support him fully! We should also tell our fellow humans who might be hurting that nothing will every separate them from the awesome love of Jesus Christ, nothing! Sometimes all individuals need to know is that they are loved and things will be fine. Dr. Johnson also provides the reader with the resources they need to connect to professionals and experts.

As one reads *Beyond Surviving: From Religious Oppression to Queer Activism,* I hope that reflection takes place in the heart and mind. I hope that the complexity of stories will be made simple through the meaning of love for one another. I hope that parents will be able to allow their children the freedom to be who they are; I am sure that we have all disappointed our parents in our choices throughout life because we are different. I also pray that individuals who are going through a difficult time will learn they are not alone. And, finally, I hope that professionals in multiple fields will take away lessons learned through the stories. However, even if one is in total disagreement with the "lifestyles of others, it is my prayer that they be compassionate and remember the following verse. Romans 8:37-39, *"Know, in all these things we are more than conquerors through him who loved us. For I am sure that neither death nor life, nor angels nor rulers, nor things present nor things to come, nor powers, nor height nor depth, nor anything else in all creation, will be able to separate us from the love of God in Christ Jesus our Lord."*

I believe we all are better equipped to work with LGBTQ individuals from coming upon Dr. Johnson's *Beyond Surviving: From Religious Oppression to Queer Activism.*

Lemuel W. Watson
Dean of the College of Education and Professor
University of South Carolina

ACKNOWLEDGEMENTS

I gratefully acknowledge the support I received from the many academic mentors I had in my life. I would like to especially thank Dr. Lemuel Watson for encouraging me to share my voice and passion through writing. I acknowledge all the LGBTQ writers and activists who came before me; I build this work upon the labors of your love. I thank those who have been in my life since the beginning and those who have recently entered and helped me finish this book; Amber Vickers, Dawn Bartolomeo, and Angela Godwhani. Roman Hailu, thank you for being my first Christian friend to fully support all of me. I would like to thank those friends who allowed me to annoyingly and endlessly talk about this research and actually listen to me; Yuma Nakada, JP Villafuerte, and Satya Chima. I would not have the passion or intellectual ability without those early times with my family as I made sense of how my identity fit within our family and in society. My family provided me with the experiences, love, support, and challenges to help me understand and articulate the stories of these students. I am blessed to have an amazing mother who always prays for me and taught me to be a uniquely confident individual, and who taught me all the critical thinking skills I ever needed. Lastly, I acknowledge my God, redeemer, and sole purpose for living, Jesus Christ. Every ounce of my compassion for helping and serving others comes from you.

CONTENTS

INTRODUCTION

This book shares the stories of Christian students in same-sex relationships as they encounter oppression, adolescence, first-love, and then a passion for social justice. Each of the students had early experiences related to family, religious, and educational socialization, which framed the ways in which they experienced their same-sex relationships as high school and college students. Although there were many positive outcomes of being in a same-sex relationship as a youth, all of the participants described internal and external conflicts that they struggled to manage. These stories are filled with attempts of suicide, physical and verbal abuse, isolation, loneliness, depression, and hospitalizations; moreover, they are also filled with triumph, self-realizations, community building, and the development of powerful queer leaders. These students turned their oppressive experiences into fuel for queer activism. The major themes focus on seeking family support, hiding loving relationships, seeking community acceptance, deconstructing socialization, and doubting the morality of their romances.

As each student struggled to overcome internal and external conflicts they relied on a variety of institutional and individual resources, which provided support to them as they attempted to resolve challenges with their religious, spiritual, and sexual identities. Some institutional support systems included university lesbian, gay, bisexual, and transgender (LGBT) campus centers, LGBT student organizations, supportive and well-informed counselors, and openly affirming churches. Some of the individual support systems included university student affairs staff members, close friends, wellness and stress management events, and media venues that positively portrayed non-heterosexual people. These students did more than just survive the oppression they faced from families, schools, the LGBT community, and religious institutions; they thrived as community and educational leaders. Through their pain they triumphed to inspire others to overcome obstacles and create change in their communities.

This book is intended for educators, parents, community organizers, religious clergy or any who might know a youth who could be LGBTQ. Higher education administrators including counselors, residence life professionals, diversity and LGBT center staff judicial affairs officers, and many other student affairs educators will gain great insight from these students' stor-ies. Educators are religious or public institutions around the country and those especially in populations with higher concentrations of Christian identified students, such as the Southeast and Midwest, should also be highly interested in understanding the experiences of Christian students in same-sex relationships.

Religious leaders such as youth group leaders, campus min-istry pastors, and even other religious leaders not within the Christian faith could greatly benefit from these students' stories of multiple aspects of marginality. Since most of the intense emotional challenges, mental health issues, and suicide attempts occurred in high school, high school teachers, administrators, counselors and parents and family members should read these students' stories.

Little is known about how Christian students experience same-sex relationships and what types of challenges they may encounter; therefore, it has proven difficult for educotors to provide appropriate support. In addition to holistically supporting LGBTQ college students, this book is also relevant to the survival of many LGBTQ youth. In the last few years there have been several notable incidents of suicides among LGBT youth.

Within a three week period during the fall of 2010, five non-heterosexual teenagers committed suicide (Hubbard, 2010). Two of the students were college students; Tyler Clementi was a student at Rutgers University who jumped to his death from the George Washington Bridge after being bullied in his residence hall about his relationship with another man (Hubbard, 2010). Raymond Chase was an openly gay student at Johnson & Wales University who hanged himself in his residence hall (Hubbard, 2010). The religious identities of these students were not discussed, but non-heterosexual students face intense emotional challenges on a college campus, and religious identity can further complicate those challenges.

It has been discussed for some time now that gay, lesbian, and bisexual people have conflicts as they begin to understand their sexuality, but Christian people usually face more challenges and higher levels of anxiety (Yip, 1997). When Christian students engage in same-sex relationships and face severe emotional conflicts, their spiritual well-being can suffer. While students are in college their spiritual well-being must be supported in order to foster holistic development. People with same-sex attractions often feel like they must choose either their religion and spirituality or their same-sex relationship (Rosser, 1992).

College students receive messages of what is "normal" from many directions (Savin-Williams, 1996) and portrayals of "normal" gay and lesbian people are mostly of those who are not religious (Poynter & Washington, 2005). In order to support all students, educators should understand the muliple dynamics that take place within students' lives. Christian students engaged in same-sex relationships may need different and additional types of support. There is little knowledge available for educators to utlize to provide adequate support to these students and few resources available to students on how to manage these conflicts, which is why this book was written. Educators and students can now better understand the experiences, challenges, and resources needed to support Christian students in same-sex relationships.

Methods

In order to capture the experiences of these students, semi-structured interviews were utilized. The interviews included a portion of pre-written open-ended questions which were asked to all participants. Semi-structured interviews were used because it was assumed that the students defined their worlds in unique ways. There are questions and issues to be discussed, but not in a particular order. Semi-structured interviews allowed the students to share their stories openly and also allowed the researcher to initiate further conversation. The interview questions can be seen in the appendix.

Each student was interviewed for 60-90 minutes on several occasions, and all of the students were given pseudonyms. The interviews were all recorded using a digital audio recorder and then each interview was transcribed. Additionally, reflective notes about observations and speculations were documented. In addition to the reflective notes, demographic details were recorded. The interviews were conducted in neutral spaces, so the students were most comfortable. I traveled to meet each participant in person, and closed office spaces in university common spaces were utilized in order to provide privacy and convenience for the students.

After each interview I would analyze the interviews and develop follow-up questions for the subsequent interviews. The students' stories and experiences were used to describe key themes and sub-themes related to the research questions. The students had to meet specific criteria in order to be invited to be involved with this project. All of the students identified as Christian or did identify as Christian when they were engaging in their same-sex relationship(s). The students were engaged in what they defined as a "dating-relationship" with someone of the same sex. A "dating-relationship" is here described as a means through which a romantic relationship is pursued, practiced, and established (Savin-Williams, 1996).

The students were currently undergraduate students or had exited their undergraduate experience within the last two years. The students were asked to reflect on their experiences as undergraduate students, so the length of time that has lapsed was minimal. The research project utilized purposeful sampling that was non-probability sampling. The students came from a variety of institutions of higher education within the United States due to the limited size and accessibility of this population. Students were recruited using institutional LGBT centers and student organizations, multicultural centers, academic departments, and by referrals.

CHAPTER 1: IDENTITY AND CONFLICT

Gay, lesbian, and bisexual people develop their identity through-out their lives, and much of that development may occur during the time they are on a college campus. Developmental theorists have created models that attempt to explain the process people would evolve through or move around in as they face society and their previously constructed identities. Although there are many theories and models explaining the experiences gay, lesbian, and bisexual people go through, this book will focus on two that are most relevant for college students. Cass's Model of Homosexual Identity Formation (1979) and D'Augelli's Model of Lesbian, Gay, and Bisexual Development (1994) are most relevant with respect to a student's development and experiences while in college.

Students in same-sex relationships have many challenges and they have to be concerned with how they express their affection for one another in public; many monitor their interactions in order to avoid harassment (Savin-Williams, 1996). Out of fear of violence or harassment, many students attempt to hide their sexual orientation (D'Augelli, 1992). In addition to students in same-sex relationships, students of color were also more likely to attempt to conceal their sexual orientation in order to avoid harassment (Rankin, 2003). When students have to hide their sexual identity it can hinder their identity development process and lead to ongoing psychological challenges (Savin-Williams, 1996).

As gay, lesbian, and bisexual students encounter oppression from numerous sources, they spend an immense amount of psycho-logical energy attempting to cope with the challenges in their lives (Savin-Williams, 1996). The development of a positive sexual identity for those attracted to the same-sex is often a long process; it took an average of eleven years for gay men between their first same-gender feelings of attraction until they could say they had a positive gay self-identity (Cohen & Savin-Williams, 1996). The emotional struggles of gay, lesbian, and bisexual youth can include feelings of depression, confusion, anxiety, and isolation. However, more severe experiences of gay, lesbian, and bisexual youth include higher rates of alcohol and drug abuse as well as suicide and suicide attempts (Burke & Stabb, 1995).

The experiences that gay, lesbian, and bisexual Christians face are diverse, complicated, and unique to each individual. Many gay, lesbian, and bisexual people hold their religious views in an important place in their lives, yet they often face struggles from multiple sources. Much of the conflict can be received from religious organizations, such as churches, Bible studies, or campus ministries. Many gay, lesbian, and bisexual people also face internal struggles related to their own spirituality and sexuality, which can lead to intense emotional issues. Gay, lesbian, and bisexual Christians must attempt to balance multiple identities, and at times these identities may seem to conflict with one another.

Religion, spirituality, and Christianity are critical pieces in the lives of many gay, lesbian, and bisexual people. The spiritual experiences of gay and lesbian people typically mirror those of heterosexual people, and many practice with traditional religious organizations (Barret & Barzan, 1996). Rosser (1991) found that 84% of gay male participants in his study were raised in some faith, but only 16% still attended; Rosser concluded that it was due to the alienation they received from religious organizations. In a recent study of examining Black men and bisexuality, the researchers reported that esteemed religion and spirituality were vital components of the participants lives, and more than half of them regularly attended church and worship services (Jeffries, Dodge, and Sandfort, 2008). Those who participate in traditional religious groups may disclose their sexuality, but many may keep it undisclosed in order to avoid rejection (Barret & Barzan, 1996).

Historically, Christian organizations have not been welcoming of non-heterosexual people; however, there are a growing number of non-heterosexual affirming churches (Schuck & Liddle, 2001) There are other Christian organizations—such as some Methodist, Episcopalian, and Presbyterian churches—that have positive views of same-sex relationships and many gay and lesbian people may choose to worship at those congregations (Barret & Barzan, 1996). Gay, lesbian, and bisexual people have previously been or currently are a part of all types of Christian churches, and conflict continues to persist in many of their lives.

For people undergoing much stress and anguish, a supportive network can be a great relief; moreover, the church often serves that role for many people. Christian people are accustomed to having a social network to support them through life's trials. However, openly gay, lesbian, and bisexual people rarely find communal support from traditional organized religious groups. There are a limited number of churches that are openly affirming of non-heterosexuals, but most churches approach gay, lesbian, and bisexual people with intolerance (Jeffries, Dodge, & Sandfort, 2006). The messages sent by churches vary, but many non-affirming churches, such as most Evangelical churches, clearly view same-sex acts as sin. Those who are a part of Evangelical churches usually receive the message that same-sex relationships are perversions and the person involved needs a transforming conversion through Jesus Christ (Bess, 1995).

According to Seow (1996), the church is to blame for the discrimination, rejection, humiliation, and high suicide rates of LGBT people. Some Christian groups have placed the cause of national tragedies, such as Hurricane Katrina and 9/11, on God's judgment of same-sex relationships (Kinnaman & Lyons, 2007). Within Black churches the rejection is often more intense; same-sex relationships in Black communities are rarely discussed and seen as an abomination. The Black church has been a place of refuge for many, yet it oppresses those people who may need it most—those who are involved with same-sex relationships (Griffin, 2006). Some gay, lesbian, and bisexual Christians believe God's love and the church's institutionalization of God's love are very different things (Tigert, 1996).

Even though many gay, lesbian, and bisexual people feel pain, alienation, and frustration from the church, they still feel it is an important part of their lives (Tigert, 1996). Gay, lesbian, and bisexual people who decide to leave their religious churches and groups due to ridicule and condemnation often feel a sense of loss and grief (Ritter & O'Neill, 1989). For many Christians, the church is a family and a spiritual support network. When individuals disconnect from a core group they can face pain and suffering. If their Christian group identity is a salient part of their identity and they lose their connection, they can experience additional crises. If gay, lesbian, and bisexual individuals abandon their Christian identity, they can also face disappointment from their families.

As gay, lesbian, and bisexual college students are attempting to find a community in which they feel they can belong, they often face rejection from multiple communities, based off of race, religion, or sexuality (Poynter & Washington, 2005). Oftentimes the most prejudiced attitudes towards gay, lesbian, and bisexual Christians are from members of the gay, lesbian, and bisexual community because they view them as antithetical to the gay movement (Swanson, 2004). There is no space on campuses to find authentic dialogue about these conflicts, so no true community is found (Poynter & Washington, 2005). If margin-alized people do not find a space where they feel welcomed they can become isolated and alienated. Gay, lesbian, and bisexual Christians face institutional oppression and rejection on multiple levels, which can lead to internal emotional and spiritual struggles.

Gay, lesbian, and bisexual Christians can feel self-hatred because they consider same-sex attraction a sin. After they repeatedly beg for God to take away their same-sex attraction and nothing changes, they can feel abandonment, guilt, and self-rejection (Bess, 1995; Griffin, 2006). If gay, lesbian, and bisexual Christians are unable to change their desires they feel unlovable and overly sinful (Ritter & O'Neill, 1989). Not only do these struggles turn into self-hatred, but they can also lead the struggling Christian to feel hatred from God (Wilcox, 2003). Schuck and Liddle (2001) found that many Christian gay, lesbian and bisexual people responded that they felt they were being sent to hell or God rejected them. As some gay and lesbian Christians begin to reject the Church they can also turn hate towards God because they feel He made them attracted to the same sex (Wilcox, 2003). As gay, lesbian, and bisexual Christians attempt to manage a range of emotions, they may choose to abandon their religion. Christian people's relationships with God are closely tied to purpose and meaning in life, so if they sever ties with God they also can feel a loss of purpose and meaning in life

RESOLVING CONFLICT

There are several studies that explain how gay, lesbian, and bisexual Christians have managed to cope with or overcome the conflict faced from religious organizations. The most prominent study describing how Christians in same-sex relationships manage conflict with a Christian organization is from Yip (1997). Yip's (1997) strategies are related to how Christians in same-sex relationships manage the stigma received from churches and Christian organizations. One strategy is Attacking the Stigma, which includes invalidating the Bible and its conventional interpretations of same-sex relations (Yip, 1997). Gay, lesbian, and bisexual Christians will develop their own interpretations of the

Bible outside of what their religious organization tells them. The second strategy is Attacking the Stigmatizer, which includes removing the church's credibility as the guardian of morality (Yip, 1997). The third strategy is Positive Personal Experience, which argues that personal experience with supportive same-sex relationships can make people better Christians (Yip, 1997). The last strategy is Ontogeneric Argument, which argues that all sexualities were created by God, so none can be wrong (Yip, 1997).

Another strategy some gay, lesbian, and bisexual Christians choose to resolve conflict is to leave Christianity, religion altogether, or their current religious organization and join a non-heterosexual affirming church (Schuck & Liddle, 2001). Leaving Christianity can be easy for some, but very difficult for others who will continue to miss their church and religious practices (Schuck & Liddle, 2001). Some participants in Schuck's and Liddle's (2001) study rejected the church and parted with it until they felt comfortable enough with their sexuality, and then returned to the church. Many people who leave organized religion and a Christian organization still identify as Christian, and practice faith individually. When churches reject gay, lesbian, and bisexual people, those excluded may focus more on spirituality than religion, which leads them to invest more in a personal relationship with God (Ritter & O'Neil, 1989). In a study by Sherry, Adleman, Whilde, and Quick (2010), they found that in order to resolve conflict, 29% of participants left their non-affirming religion for an affirming religion, 11% of participants rejected God and religion, and 12% of participants continued their religious practices but still felt guilt and shame.

Compartmentalization was another method that some gay, lesbian, and bisexual people used to help them manage conflict. In Jeffries', Dodge's, and Sanfrot's (2008) study on Black bisexual men, they found that many of the participants developed strategies to balance only one identity at a time in order to avoid a stigma being attached to them. These men continued involvement with their churches and had female partners, but also had relationships with other men without the church knowing (Jeffries, Dodge, & Sandfort, 2008). Religion, sexuality, and spirituality are nonetheless integral parts of a person, so compartmentalization can lead to stress (Yip, 1996; Tigert, 1996)

As gay, lesbian, and bisexual Christians face a multitude of struggles—including depression, anxiety, isolation, and self-hatred (Bess, 1995; Seow, 1996, Yip, 1997)—they must attempt to resolve the conflict. One of the initial attempts many Christians make is to pray and beg for God to change them or give them strength to overcome same-sex attractions; however, when people cannot overcome the same-sex attraction—even with repeated prayers, pleas, and therapy—they can feel loneliness, fear, guilt, and self-rejection (Bess, 1995; Griffin, 2006). In Schuck's and Liddle's (2001) study participants reported that when they approached clergy with their conflict the clergy encouraged them to pray for forgiveness. The same study's participants also stated that their gay, lesbian, and bisexual friends were positive resources and seeing a therapist was helpful (Schuck & Liddle, 2001).

Although counseling has been stated to be helpful for gay, lesbian, and bisexual Christians seeking conflict resolution, it can be difficult finding a counselor who is prepared to address the complex struggles with religion, spirituality, and sexuality. When gay and lesbian Christians who are struggling with conflict seek out professional assistance from counselors they can also be faced with more adversity. If they seek out a Christian counselor they can often feel more condemnation, judgment, or pressure to conform to the counselor's interpretations of the Bible (Levine & Love, 2000). When gay and lesbian Christians seek help from secular mental health professionals they can also find their pain intensified. Many mental health professionals are not prepared to understand complex issues with spirituality. When mental health profession-als approach the situations with ignorance of the pain and unique searching of gay and lesbian spirituality they can hinder the journey towards identity synthesis and self-actualization (Ritter & O'Neill, 1989).

In order to manage internal strife from conflicting feelings on religion and sexuality, the men in Jeffries, Dodge, and Sandfort's (2008) study relied on their own form of spirituality and questioned the sanctions of organized religion; spirituality was a prominent coping mechanism against negative internal emotions and hostility from the church. They began to look at sexuality in a more naturalistic perspective that presumed their sexual orien-tation was designed by God (Jeffries, Dodge, and Sandfort, 2008). When these men faced challenges from the church and in life they relied on God; they reported that he served as their protector from danger, hardship, and death (Jeffries, Dodge, and Sandfort, 2008). God also helped them cope with emotional struggles, physical pain, and sexual abuse (Jeffries, Dodge, and Sandfort, 2008).

Chapter 2: Joshua, Experiences and Motivation

Beginning this project was not pleasant or easy. It actually terrified me, and I tried to quit numerous times. The battles I had in my head, heart, and spirit for years surfaced when my advisor asked me to collaborate on a research project about gays and Christians. Although I knew someone should write about this topic, I did not want that person to be me. At the age of 25, I had never reconciled my same-sex attractions with my spiritual and religious lives. Two months after I first became romantic with another man, I embarked upon an academic adventure exploring how Christian students experienced same-sex relationships. My journey is on-going, and this project has forced me to examine my multiple conflicting identities. The isolation and condemnation I faced turned me into a compassionate educator, fully-devoted Christian, and professional queer activist. As I examined each person's story, I processed my own.

As with any qualitative project, the researcher becomes the instrument. Although I aimed to remain unbiased, my life experiences frame how I heard their stories and what I felt was relevant when telling their stories. There were numerous methods used to ensure these stories are credible and relevant, but with all research there are limitations. I am honored to be able to tell their stories, and these are their stories from my perspective. In order to better understand the following stories of sadness, pain, and hope, one must first know the story of the writer. My story is still evolving, and I continue to resolve the issues with my identity. I give many thanks to the students who allowed me to grow as a researcher, educator, and person through hearing and retelling their stories.

BACKGROUND

I was raised by protestant Christian ministers, and became a born-again Christian at the early age of eleven. From that time on until the present, I define the center of my life as a personal relationship with Jesus Christ. I was trained from an early age to believe that the Bible was the guide for my life and the direction stated in it should not be questioned. I was socialized from an early age by religious and parental teachings that romantic same-sex relationships were sinful abominations and socially unacceptable. Religious socialization also occurred through primary education because I was home-schooled until high school with an evangelical Christian curriculum. From birth, Christian ideology was a part of my life, and my loving parents' sole purpose in life was to raise solid evangelical Christians.

My perspectives are also framed by my racial identity as a multiracial Korean-American and European person. My Korean-American mother converted to Christianity and it was not long until my White-American father joined her at church. Before I was even born they were on the church staff, and before I was a teenager they were ordained ministers. My racial identity prepared me to understand what it was like to be an outsider.

Growing up in Mississippi, I never saw others who looked like me, and even within my own family I felt like an outsider. With two older brothers and two older sisters, I straddled the middle of masculine and feminine. My gender expression always excluded me from fully fitting into one gender category. As I struggled to understand my racial identity and gender expression, I also had to face the truth that I was also attracted to men.

At the age of fifteen I realized I was attracted to other boys or men. I never knew gay or non-heterosexual people, so it was almost like a fantasy world. It was not reality, and there were no options of romantic involvement even if I wanted. Around this same time I began to focus my life much more on spiritual growth, and the one sin I always focused on "fixing" was my same-sex attraction. For nearly ten years my prayers revolved around on-going repentance because I was attracted to other men Shame, guilt, and disappointment plagued my emotions. It was hard to stay focused on actively serving God because I spent so much time trying to not have attractions towards other men.

Throughout my youth and adulthood I have been active within Christian churches. Church was my home and the first place I found when I moved to a new city; within the last the years I have lived in six different cities. Since I hold my church family in such a significant part of my life, it was often there were I was hurt the most. The first time I recall feeling the pain of condemnation was when I was 17. I belonged to a small church of about 50 people, so everyone knew each other very well. I grew up with these people and spent three to four days a week with them.

As we sat in the congregation talking after service, my friend, Carlene (pseudonym), and I were having a conversation. She made a comment and I disagreed. Carlene's response was, "Don't roll your eyes at me you faggot." The shame and hatred I had towards myself surfaced through her words. Those few words made me feel isolated and hated in the only place I thought I was safe.

His word, "faggot," plagued my life. Just as I was discovering that I had these attractions, I remember my dad seeing a feminine man on television and he exclaimed, "fag." It was not directed at me, but it made me fear that my dad would hate me if he ever knew. This was not the first or only time these words left my father's lips. My mom was compassionate and I was her baby boy. She always wants the best for me and has nothing but love. The love she has is centered on me serving God whole-heartedly, marrying a godly woman, and producing little Christian soldiers. We rarely talked about homosexuality when I was growing up, but the times we did, I left with the understanding that being a homosexual was because one was damaged and demonized; with enough prayer, fasting, and Bible study one would be free.

As I hit young adulthood, graduated college, and moved to my "big city" of Birmingham, Alabama I found a church. After months of gaining many new friends, mostly female, I felt at home. As I grew closer to several men in the church, I realized I was not welcome there if I was not heterosexual. One of my casual friends, Justin (pseudonym), told me he did not talk to me for the first few months because he thought I was weird. Later he explained that by "weird" he meant gay. I was not openly identifying with any sexual orientation at that time, but I knew that this group would not include me if I was not heterosexual. I am fortunate to have avoided any severe incidents of physical or verbal assaults. My pain came in the form of fearing that people would know I had this attraction and abandon me forever. My fear led to isolation, shallow friendships, and a life full of shame.

RELATIONSHIP

From the ages of 16-21, I chose to not be involved with anyone romantically; neither women nor men. I was focusing on my relationship with God, which largely included trying to rid myself of all same-sex attractions. At the age of twenty-two I admitted to someone other than myself that I was not heterosexual. I was now in a graduate program and taking a class on black families. The instructor was queer-identified and I had to write a paper on my identity, including my sexuality. I felt safe with the professor and he was one of the first queer people I remember knowing. From this point on I began to feel comfortable admitting I was attracted to men, but felt it would be sinful to become physically involved with men. Over the next few years I learned about my insecurities and fears, socialization, identity, and intersectionality. I still focused much of my prayer time on trying to resist any temptation to become involved with a man. My life's purpose had been consumed by one rule; do not be with a man.

At twenty-five I met a man that made me break that rule. The next nine months of my life was turmoil. I am usually focused and disciplined with my academics, career, physical fitness, eating healthy, spirituality, and even romantic involvement. As I realized my relationship with Alex (pseudonym) was more than just friends I grew excited, but fearful at the same time. After months of being just friends, we became more than just friends. Guilt and shame caused me to cut him off; then go back to him in an ongoing and painful cycle. I struggled to be in the same room with him at times, and would make him leave or lock myself in my bedroom. After four months of spending time getting to know each other, I once again told him it was over. I could not handle disappointing God because I was with a man. Not only was I confused and conflicted, but I was also feeling the pain of losing a friend and romance. I also had to deal with the guilt of hurting someone I truly cared for. As I tried to figure out my identities I routinely put myself in pain while dragging romantic interests into a mess of emotions and hurt. I still have deep regrets for causing Alex immense pain as I tried to figure out my identities.

During this highly emotional time of trying to figure out what was right and wrong, I felt I had no one who I could trust to share my conflicts with. Most of close friends were evangelical Christians, and I knew their views on same-sex relationships. The stigma of any type of same-sex feelings was intense, and I did not trust anyone in my Christian groups to seek support from. At this point in my life I had never met a Christian person who espoused any positive ideals about non-heterosexual people. I did talk to one of my non-Christian friends; however, she told me to just ignore all that Christian ideology and Biblical text. She tried to help me with my struggles, but she did not understand the role of religion and spirituality in my life. I often wanted to seek professional counseling, but I could not figure who to go to. I was reading Exodus International books focused on healing people with same-sex attractions, and they recommended finding an Exodus International counselor in my area. I even feared talking with a Christian counselor specializing in ex-gay therapy because I knew they would look at me as diseased. I did not trust talking with a non-Christian counselor because I have always felt that many counselors are anti-Christian. I struggled to find someone who grasped my spiritual identity and my sexual identity. Shame, fear, and loneliness filled my life for months.

RESOLVING

Through all of the rejection, isolation, and condemnation I have received from my birth family and church family, I never once fell into depression, self-hatred, self-mutilation or had suicidal ideations. I attribute my resilience to my on-going relationship with Jesus Christ. The emotional distress I faced was minimal compared to others, and I was able to overcome because of my understanding of what Christianity and religion meant to me. Prior to any same-sex attraction I viewed my religion and spirituality as a relationship with God and not with an organization, family, culture, or book. It was hurtful to face condemnation from my family and church, and after a few moments of self-pity I would pray. I was always put at peace and reminded that those people's words are not God's words.

I attribute my ability to balance a (now) healthy holistic identity to my critical thinking skills. My mother raised me to be highly critical of world perspectives. I was taught school at home because my parents did not agree with public school curriculum. I was not allowed to listen to non-Christian music because the lyrics and artists were promoting unchristian values. From an early age I was taught to critically analyze forms of socialization from school and media. Those skills that my mother taught me became useful as the Church and my mother's interpretation of scripture made me feel dirty and unable to fulfill my purpose. As I began to attempt to make sense of being someone with same-sex attractions I turned to many forms of knowledge, including conservative Christian media as well as secular social science research. Through on-going research, prayer, and reflection, I was able to come to a place where I accepted all of my identities.

As I began conducting research on Christian students in same-sex relationship I was forced to think about my conflicts. I am an expert at placing conflict and emotions in a special hiding place where no one goes; however, spending numerous hours each week reading about this conflict and listening to others' experiences always brought my conflict to the surface. I attribute my self-acceptance to this book, to these students' stories, and to my mentor who made me do this project. I presented early findings of this project at a national conference after the first year of conducting research, and my advisor stated that he was aware that I had many emotions going into the presentation. As we continued, I grew to further understand my relationship with Christ and others. Several years later, I watched the film *Fish Out of Water*, and it challenge my ways in which I studied the Bible. During that summer, the pastor at my church also discussed ways in which to read the Bible; I began to learn more about how to study the Bible in regards to culture, context, and interpretation.

I would love to say that I had mobs of people rallying to support me and understand this conflict present within my core; however I was usually alone. Even when I trusted someone enough to expose the hurt and confusion inside, they did not understand. This conflict was overwhelmingly difficult for me to articulate, thus even more difficult for an outsider to understand. Through feeling like an outsider in my racial identity and gender expression, I had become comfortable not having a group. My racial identity was misunderstood; my gender expression never met others' standards; and then my sexuality was deemed sinful and my religious identity was deemed oppressive. I could not wait for someone to affirm me and my identity. I had to seek out multiple perspectives, make a decision for myself on what I believed, and avoid letting others push me out of spaces that I knew I belonged in.

Through and on-going commitment to figuring myself out, critical thinking skills, and never letting anything get between me and my relationship with Jesus; I have gone beyond surviving. I am an advocate and supporter of all students, but I am honored to focus my student development efforts on queer, lesbian, gay, bisexual, pansexual, and transgender students. As I moved into my current position as a director of an LGBT center, I cried uncontrollably for hours. That moment was the release of years of pain, shame, and condemnation. My process is not done. To say that I have rid my mind of a lifetime of socialization to disapprove of LGBTQ people would be a lie; but each day I strive to love all people as Jesus loves them. I now view my role as a director of an LGBT center as my spiritual purpose. I aim to provide support, care, and love to those who have been hurt by society, their birth families, and their religious families. As painful and long as my journey has been thus far, I would not wish for any different past. My experiences and identity have motivated me to welcome, support, and advocate for those coming from all marginalized backgrounds.

CHAPTER 3: TYLER, THE DEMONS WITHIN

As a 19 year old college sophomore, Tyler (a pseudonym provided by the participant) faced challenges and grew tremendously as he encountered oppression and hatred from family,
religion, and society. As a Black—Tyler explicitly identified as
black and not African-American—gay identified Baptist Christian, he grew up in a mostly black community in Chicago,
Illinois and attended a large public institution near where he
grew up. Through numerous external and internal conflicts,
Tyler turned to his boyfriend, Andy, as a source of support. Tyler
thanked God and viewed his relationship with Andy as a gift
from God; however, their relationship was not free of obstacles.
Tyler came-out in high school several times and faced extreme
challenges from his mother and church congregation; these
struggles framed his current experiences as well as his goals
related to his life's purpose and career. Tyler's relationship with
Andy was a significant part of his life and he had tremendous
hopes that his family would be able to approve and support his
same-sex relationship.

BACKGROUND: CONDEMNED TO HELL

Tyler was raised primarily by his mother and had a distant
relationship with his father, who lived hours away in a homeless
shelter at the time of the interview. Tyler can recall as a young
child being attracted to male television show characters, but felt
it was wrong, abnormal, and sinful, so he hid these feelings
during his adolescent years. At the age of 16 Tyler came-out—
told his mom he thought he was gay— but they prayed in order
to make it go away. After a year of no longer identifying as gay,
he came-out again to his mom, and later that night woke to her
praying and attempting to cast the demons of homosexuality out
of him. Later that year, Tyler began living a double life as he

secretly became romantically involved with a male and hid it from his mom.

Tyler's relationship with his mom greatly affected his self-identity, self-acceptance, and religious and spiritual life. Tyler's mom consistently tried to remove the demons from her son through repeated prayer and Bible readings. Tyler's mom brought him to a prophet at church who told him there was a demon of perversion in him that needed to be cast out. Since Tyler's behavior did not change, his mom decided it needed to be a church matter. Tyler described what he called his "exorcism in the following narrative:

During praise and worship...my mom stood up and said to the pastor, 'My son needs prayer. He has a homosexual demon that is attacking him...' The pastor said, 'Bring him up to the altar.' My mom grabbed my hand and dragged me to the altar... Everyone in the church came up to the altar. I will never forget, the pastor came and put his hands on my head and then he told everyone to come put their hands on me and help bless me and pray for me. I started crying and they thought it was the demon. I was like no, here are 200 people coming after me to put their hands on me. Like it was horrible...I was crying. Everyone was over me, holding me, praying. Nobody could hear me. I had scratches on my arm...It didn't feel too good to have everyone praying to turn you into someone you're not. Then on top of that, them praying to take a demon out of you when nothing is there. Like praying to take my soul out of me. I still have anxiety about going into churches because of that situation.

This event greatly affected Tyler's religious and spiritual identity as he was fearful to enter a church without anxiety. Both his mom and his church community condemned his sexual orientation using the Bible as a tool to prove to him that his life was sinful and he was destined for hell. As Tyler faced intense condemnation and rejection from his mom and his church community, his internal struggles intensified. Tyler believed the messages he received from his mom and his church, and began to plead to God to remove the demons from him. The fear of being gay and being condemned to hell lead him to feel self-hatred. Tyler hated himself and begged for his same-sex attractions to leave, but the attractions would not leave. Tyler began to struggle with severe depression, and began to cut himself in order to punish himself. He hoped the physical cutting would also release the demons from his body.

Tyler's self-hatred and depression escalated as he began to contemplate suicide. Tyler described one of the lowest points of his struggle:

I started to self-mutilate because I felt I wanted to get it out of me. I thought if I would cut myself or something it would go away or if I punished myself it would go away or something like that. I don't know what I thought. It was just a really dark time...There was this freeway bridge and I ran all the way by there... I looked down and I thought about doing something. I thought about ending it. I thought about taking all the misery out and then my morality checked in and said you can't go to heaven if you do suicide. No matter how much it pained me, I didn't want to go on.

As Tyler faced self-hatred and suicidal thoughts he had no one to support or guide him. After contemplating suicide he called his mom for help, but she further condemned him and physically assaulted him. Tyler described his mom's reaction:

I told my mom where I was. She came and picked me up in the car and she sat me down in the bathroom and threw the Bible at me. Just threw it. Threw the Bible at me and told me to start reading. She told me to read the scripture where it says if man lies with another man how it is dirty and unclean and all this other garbage I refuse to believe anymore...I don't know what possessed me to show her my arms...and tell her about the self-mutilation and that I needed some help. She got the knife and she decided to cut my arm and she told me, 'If you want to cut yourself I'm going to give it to you.' So she cut my arm. I ran away...

Through all of Tyler's conflicts and challenges from his mom, church, and himself, he felt extreme isolation. Although his emotional distress was largely caused by his mom he still wanted her support and approval. Tyler had a complicated relationship with his mother that involved fear, hatred, love, and a desire for acceptance and approval. His isolation left him longing for a community and someone to support him as he encountered numerous life challenges.

RELATIONSHIP: FINDING REFUGE WITH A PARTNER

As Tyler faced numerous challenges towards the end of high school and moving into college he began a relationship with Andy. Andy was Tyler's first and only same-sex relationship. Tyler was excited to have someone to share his life with and felt deeply connected to someone in all aspects, including his religious identity. After three years of beginning their relationship they were still together and sharing a residence hall room on campus. Andy was there with Tyler since he first came-out to his family and encountered extreme family and personal trials. Tyler's opinion of their relationship was that it was a gift from God and the means by which God had provided for him. Tyler encountered challenges in his life and the one person to always support him was Andy; however, his family did not recognize the emotional support he gained from his same-sex relationship.

Andy was the only person who helped Tyler through some of the darkest times in his life. After Tyler was physically assaulted and emotionally abused by his mom, he ran away to Andy's house. Shortly after going back home, Tyler had an emotional breakdown and ended up in the hospital. Andy remained the primary support system through the entire process. During Tyler's first year, he and Andy were not at the same school, but Andy would come to visit every weekend. Tyler was still facing intense depression and Andy was the only person there for him. Tyler had negative side effects from the medicines prescribed to him to assist with his depression, so he quit taking them and would then struggle with a variety of mixed moods and emotions. As Tyler was alone in college, Andy would come to just let him rest on him and cry. Each Sunday when it was time for Andy to leave him, Tyler felt emotionally overwhelmed because he knew he had to go five days without his boyfriend and support system. Through his relationship he has learned to love himself and accept himself. Tyler described how Andy has helped him:

I have become more confident. I love myself now and back then I didn't. I didn't love myself at all because I was taught to be disgusted with myself and Andy helped me love myself too, which I don't see how someone loving me can be so bad. He accepted all of me from the little things, the little faults. He accepts it all, everything, which is so awesome.

Andy also identified as Christian and the two of them have been the spiritual support for one another. Since Tyler was fearful to engage in Christian organizations, he and Andy spent time reading and praying together at home. They wanted to keep God at the center of their relationship and live according to His plan. Tyler was insistent about not being physically involved with Andy until they knew they were going to be together; it was nearly a year before Tyler lost his virginity to Andy. Tyler wanted their relationship to be an example of a successful gay Christian relationship. When Tyler decided that he would be with a man he prayed to God to bring him a husband. Tyler planned to marry Andy and spend the rest of his life with him.

Being a Christian college student and being in a same-sex relationship has not been easy for Tyler. Others saw his relationship as evil and condemned by God. Tyler longed to be a part of a spiritual community, but feared their rejection of him and his relationship. Tyler knew there were churches and religious organizations that supported same-sex relationships, but his past experiences kept him from feeling welcomed and comfortable in churches. Tyler and Andy hoped to soon begin exploring more congregations in order to find a church home. Tyler gained spiritual support from the church community and longed to one day be a part of it again. Music and singing were ways in which Tyler expressed himself, as well as worshiped God; however, he no longer had the option to be a part of these groups because of his same-sex relationship.

Although Tyler viewed his relationship with Andy as a great asset to his life, most of his family did not. Tyler's mom still had difficulties accepting his sexuality and his relationship with Andy. Tyler hoped to one day have them meet and be welcomed in her home, but she refused to mention or meet him. Tyler explained further:

She (Tyler's mom) used to refer to Andy as 'that boy' or 'that person.' She can say his name without having that cringed look on her face. She used to say 'that boy' and you could see the utter disgust on her face.... She is tolerant and that is all I can ask for...It was hard for me because my family doesn't want to sit down with him or get to know him. I know that was one thing that really crushed my spirit and I had to get over. It felt incomplete and I felt guilty. It is like your family is erasing him.

Tyler was patient with his mom and saw progress; he one day hoped to have her come to a dinner at the future home he and Andy hoped to live in. Tyler viewed his mom as tolerant since she had changed from her previous reactions in his life, which were violent and verbally abusive. Tyler's mother was still not accepting of the idea of same-sex relationships or Tyler being with Andy. Although Tyler's mother did not overtly reject Andy by physically or verbally assaulting Tyler or Andy, she was still not tolerant of the idea of them being in a relationship. Although Tyler had encountered tremendous condemnation from his mom, her opinion of him and his relationship was a central part of his life and identity.

Tyler had been rejected by his family, his church, and his religious student organizations. The relationship he had with Andy was his refuge. For the last three years Andy had been his family, his support, his hope, and his encouragement. Tyler relied on Andy for all of his support as a student, Christian, partner, friend, and family. The relationship between Tyler and Andy had become the core of Tyler's life, but when Tyler needed someone to process his relationship with there were limited outlets. Tyler often felt like there was no one to go to who could help him sort out his relationship complications.

RESOLVING: BUILDING A PERSONAL RELATIONSHIP WITH GOD

Most of the conflicts surrounding Tyler's and Andy's relationship were related to his own process of reconciling his religious and sexual identities. The depression Tyler faced in the relationship had much to do with his on-going feelings of guilt, shame, and self-hatred because of his sexual orientation. At one of Tyler's lowest points when he was hospitalized for depression and suicidal ideations, he met a hospital staff member who significantly changed his outlook on religion and sexuality. Tyler described how that interaction changed his life:

I met this doctor or not a doctor, but the people in the office... he said 'You are going to be OK. You are just slowed down right now...no matter what happens, just remember that God made you this way'... He came out and told me I will get through and I just need to pray about it and he introduced me to that state of mind, that you know you didn't choose this and you know you have always been like this; then you should know God made you this way for a reason and you should accept who you are... He introduced me to that and encouraged me to explore my religion more... and actually start reading my Bible again... That is going to be there with me for the rest of my life.

Tyler changed his thoughts drastically by having one person in his life tell him it was God's plan and that he could be gay and Christian. Early in Tyler's life he prayed regularly to be free of his same-sex desires. Tyler described how his prayers changed:

I used to pray before I came out it was "God please take this away from me. It is not in your will"... I was practicing this religion from zero all the way to sixteen and believing, "Oh my gosh I am going to hell because I'm gay. I'm horrible. I have a demon in me, and all this other crap." Now I have to breakdown my whole morality and start from scratch. It was a long way. I made it a long way to accept who I am... I am telling the creator it is not in His will. I do not know what His will is...Like you can't see or touch or take a part of me away, what He instilled in me and how He made me. I was asking Him to take a part of me away. That is as bad as committing suicide...When I came to that realization my prayers changed to, "Please help me to accept me for me. Please let me accept who I am and be strong in who I am and I know you made me this way"... I started talking to God, and praying more...

As Tyler began to reframe his relationship with God he was better able to share a healthy relationship with Andy. They began to gain different perspectives on Christianity and sexuality. The Bible was used to condemn his sexual orientation and relationship; therefore, Andy and Tyler spent time reading the Bible and exploring a variety of interpretations of scriptures on same-sex relationships. Tyler learned to critically read the Bible, which allowed him to have a new perspective on his relationship with Andy.

One of the major conflicts Tyler faced was feeling isolated from his family and it was challenging for him to not have their approval or support. Tyler's mom did become more tolerant of Tyler's sexuality in his perspective. Her change in reaction came through her experience with breast cancer. Tyler returned home and was the only one to support her during her recovery process. Although he had been deeply hurt by her, he chose to forgive and support her, as he described in an interview:

She changed a lot because of the breast cancer... I was going to fight to make sure she is OK... I immediately grabbed her hand and began praying... Over the course of that summer we got so close because she was vomiting and the nausea and everything and her hair falling out... I was there... I think that put things in perspective for her greatly when it came to who I am. I think that is why she is as tolerant as she is. She is like "I may not agree with that, but he is still my son." Plus I know she found a new respect for me because of all the stuff she did, but I still stuck by her...

Through Tyler's mom's illness she was able to interact with her son in a different manner and he felt as if he was able to show that one can be Christian and gay. Tyler had moments where he did not want to forgive her for what she did to him, but tried to act as Christ would and support his mom regardless of how she treated him.

Throughout this process Andy was the biggest support for Tyler. Andy's family provided some support to them and Tyler had one sister who was supportive of their relationship. Initially, Tyler's sister told him that he was going to go to hell, but after some time she became the only family member who supported Tyler and Andy. Tyler and Andy also gained support from the university's lesbian, gay, bisexual, and transgender (LGBT) center as well as the LGBT student organization on campus. Tyler had gone to a number of counselors throughout his life, and as he transitioned to college he continued seeing counselors who allowed him to explore new ideas and perspectives.

As Tyler faced his most severe conflicts, God was the most significant method of coping and reason for overcoming. As he contemplated suicide and as he faced severe condemnation, he turned to his faith in order to survive. Tyler described how God helped him:

Through the coming out process I know there is a God. If there wasn't I wouldn't be here (laugh). I really don't think if it was for my faith I would have survived. I wouldn't have survived at all...That is who I go to for my problems and where I find comfort... There is so much that He has given us. He made sure we were safe. He got Andy here. He made sure I stayed in school My freshman year I failed all of my classes. I was on academic probation. I was going to get kicked out... Without so much prayer and being able to talk to Him on a spiritual level I would not have resolved it (conflicts with sexuality).

All of the resources and people supporting Tyler and his relationship were attributed as gifts from God. Tyler remained positive through his struggles and felt he grew from all of his conflict.
Tyler was forced to examine his religion and faith on a deeper level. As he removed himself from his church he was able to focus on his relationship with God outside of an organization. Tyler still longed for approval from his mom and family, but he was able to see his religious identity and God's love and acceptance outside of his mom's views of Christianity and same-sex relationships. As Tyler visited counselors and saw how they assisted him, he had a better understanding of his purpose in life.

Tyler was committed to helping others by becoming a counselor that addressed issues of sexual orientation and identity.

Tyler began making strides towards his goal of becoming a counselor even in his second year of college. In addition to being highly involved in the campus LGBT group he was also selected to be a peer mentor to queer and questioning students. Each week Tyler meets with students online to help them understand their gender and sexual identity. This has been Tyler's form of activism. He helped students one at a time with challenges he often faced first hand. Tyler saw his work with the LGBT center and LGBT student group as just the beginning of his advocacy for LGBT people.

Chapter 4: Eric, From Exorcisms to Oprah

Deconstructing Socialization

Eric (a pseudonym provided by the participant) can easily be described as a fighter; he does not give up easily and actively sought to change what he disliked or disagreed with. He recently finished his undergraduate degree at a Christian college in Southern California and was in a religious studies graduate program on the East coast. Eric was a Latino identified gay Christian and lived with his domestic partner, who was also named Eric. Eric spent the first part of his college life believing his religious socialization and fighting his same-sex attractions, but later changed to begin fighting the institutions and social structures that told him his same-sex relationship was wrong. As Eric and his partner encountered a variety of challenges they came together to actively confront their oppressors. Although Eric puts forth a strong stance against systems that were against same-sex relationships, he still had doubts if his relationship was pleasing to God.

Background: Fighting the Demons

As Eric grew up he was taunted because of his feminine gender expression and was assumed to be gay. Eric denied this identity because he viewed being gay as sinful. After ending his engagement to a woman at the age of 18, he pondered who he wanted to marry and could only think of it being a man. Eric was a freshman at a Christian institution and refused to accept an identity as a gay or bisexual man, so he began going to therapy in order to remove his same-sex attractions. Eric had been socialized from an early age that being gay was sinful and against God's will. It was against the college's policy to be in a same-sex relationship, so he did not want anyone at his school to know that he had desires to be with men. In an effort to try to change his same-sex attractions, he would drive to his hometown church and receive the therapy.

For over a year Eric did all he could to fight his attraction to other men. His church community taught him that his feelings were from a poor relationship with his father and could be fixed. Eric's therapy focused on him building positive relationships with other men and with his parents. Eric further described his therapy:

So I reached out to my youth pastors in my old church. We talked about these attractions and not knowing what to do... I was given male mentors who were supposed to be pseudo-father figures to me...I started going to counseling and that lasted for about a year. At the end of that I was having a lot of trouble and was on the verge of suicide... That was never reaffirmed by my pastor that I was still loved by God. For some reason that was what made me want to end my life thinking that God did not love me. I put God and my relationship with God before everything else...I don't think there was ever a time when I felt like it was working. I didn't always believe that it was going to work, but I never felt like it was a waste. I would go to bed every night angry and ticked off, yelling at God which would then turn into me crying and blaming God.

During therapy Eric struggled to know if God still loved him and that drove him to keep trying to change. Eric viewed his relationship with God as the most important part of his life, and he viewed the church and its leadership as messengers from God. After a year of regular therapy his same-sex desires were not fading. At Eric's last attempt to change he followed the pastor's advice to have a deliverance meeting to get the demons out of him. He explained further:

A lot of spiritual warfare was going on and demons in my life. They wanted to pray a deliverance over me...I was like sure, great that is what we have to do. I felt vulnerable and that what they said was true... That following Thursday him and three other men from the church came. We talked about why we were there and they sat me down on a chair and they started praying over me; putting olive oil on my head. About an hour or an hour and a half, I had flung out of my chair and on the ground and was speaking in tongues...There was a bucket under my chair where they were hoping I would vomit up the demon in me... It was after that experience that I never went back there. I felt so empty and depressed after that. I accepted the fact that I was not going to change, but I was not happy with that. I felt like I am not going to change and God is not going to love me.

Eric gave up fighting to change and wanted to embrace his identity as a non-heterosexual man. Eric believed all that the church had told him and had followed their instructions, but the results he was hoping for never happened. Eric tried all that he could to remove his same-sex attractions, but each attempt left him feeling more hopeless. He was skeptical of the deliverance process, but had some hope that it would remove his desire to be with other men. Eric described the counseling and deliverance experiences as spiritual for him, but they were exhausting and did not provide his expected outcomes. As Eric realized his same-sex feelings were not going away, he changed his intentions, and wanted to be able to embrace those feelings and accept his sexual identity. However, as he accepted his identity as a bisexual man and later as a gay man, he also associated bisexual and gay identities with anti-Christian identities. He felt he had to choose his sexual identity or his religious identity, and at this point in his life he was choosing his sexual identity. Eric began to deconstruct messages the church had taught him, but he still struggled to deconstruct other societal messages, such as those that exclude religion from the lives of non-heterosexual people.

As Eric began to explore his sexual identity outside of his church and religious college, he struggled to understand what it meant to be gay. Eric wanted to embrace his identity as a gay man, but his views of gay men were narrow and negative. Eric explained his feelings further:

I accepted I was not going to change. But I did not think it was pleasing to God; it did not fit with being a Christian. I was just going to be gay. My perception of what it meant to be gay was totally messed up. What I was told about how gay people acted, I thought they were promiscuous party animals who got HIV and AIDS and died. So I thought that is what I am going to become. I was going to be a party boy. Even when I felt like this I thought why would anybody want this? That is when I went into depression. This is how I am going to live the rest of my life and die and go to hell. Why wait, I should just end it now.

As Eric was trying to reconcile his sexual and religious identities he found himself in many risky situations—having sex with random people in an emotionless state, which he disliked. As Eric went back to his college he sought to find a community and found Eric who listed his identity on Facebook as gay and Christian. Eric and Eric began a relationship soon after Eric finished his ex-gay therapy. As Eric stopped trying to fight his same-sex attractions he began fighting his religious institution and societal messages that told him his sexual identity and relationship were wrong.

RELATIONSHIP: FIGHTING INSTITUTIONAL OPPRESSION

Eric was planning on committing suicide because he did not like what he thought he would become as he claimed a gay identity. Eric assumed he was going to hell and decided he would just end it now instead of waiting; however, Eric received a message from Eric, which included a Bible verse about God always loving him. This verse brought a new revelation to Eric and gave him hope of reconciling his identities. When Eric got back to his campus he met Eric for the first time and after one date they decided to be in a relationship. Their relationship made Eric happier and it was the beginning of his on-going process of reconciliation. However, Eric still had many negative views of his relationship from a lifetime of negative socialization. Eric explained further:

The relationship started just after my exorcism... Confusion, I can sum it up in one word... I went from trying to change myself and then going into a relationship with a man. I had thoughts that I was a sinner and needed to change; they were thoughts and feelings of sinful, wrong, unnatural. It was hard for both of us and we had to process it together. We read the Bible since we just got into this relationship and tried to figure out what it was.

Eric was dealing with many personal challenges which affected his relationship with another man. His partner was also dealing with a variety of emotions related to his religious and sexual identities as they began their relationship.

In addition to interpersonal and internal struggles, Eric also dealt with fighting his institution's views on same-sex relationships. Eric shared:

We were at a Christian college where we had a policy that said homosexual or same-sex relationships were wrong and against the policy. It was hard being a couple. We had chapel three times a week. We would be sitting there three times a week together... When I would walk him home from my apartment we would hide behind cars to kiss good night and there was always this paranoia that we would out ourselves and someone would find out, and then we would get kicked out.

Eric and his partner were fearful of their relationship being discovered which caused great stress as they managed their academics, personal life, and examined their spiritual lives. Eventually both of them left the institution after the dean told them to either withdraw or be expelled. After transferring to a public institution in California, they still faced challenges in their relationship. Eric aimed to live in family housing with his partner, but the policies were heteronormative and it was a lengthy process to prove that they were in a legal partnership. Once they were living together there was still the fear of facing hate and discrimination from staff who would find out they were living together as a couple.

Eric and his partner endured these struggles from a variety of institutions, but they continued to fight in order to change institutions and policies. After being together for several years, Eric still had to fight his own feelings about their relationship. He actively challenged policies that told them their relationship was unacceptable, but he also actively challenged himself and his views on their relationship. Eric shared, "Part of me asks this question of 'What if?' What if I am wrong? What if God does not like it?'" The struggles of being in a same-sex relationship were complex for Eric and included both internal and external challenges, whose resolution was on-going and lengthy.

RESOLVING: OVERCOMING THROUGH ACTIVISM

Eric continued to process his ongoing struggles related to his sexual and religious identities, and his relationship aided him to process these challenges. Eric and his partner spent time early in their relationship examining the Bible and discussing how their religious life and relationship affected each other. They supported one another and were able to develop the language to also discuss the topic with other people. As they examined the Bible, they began to read it more critically and would place more focus on the life of Jesus and his messages. Reading the Bible with a critical lens was beneficial as they aimed to deconstruct a lifetime of socialization they received from many sources. In addition to receiving support from his partner, Eric also joined an online forum for gay Christians where he was able to share

46

and engage in a different community. Eric's academic work within religious studies exposed him to a variety of topics and he used his writing projects to process his conflict. A book by Jack Rogers, *Jesus, the Bible, and Homosexuality*, was instrumental in assisting Eric process his internal conflict of having negative views of same-sex relationships and identifying as gay. Combating a lifetime of socialization took many tools and much time to overcome.

As Eric aimed to surmount the challenges of hiding his relationship at a Christian college, he quickly became an activist. He and Eric went to Los Angeles to protest the military's policy on Don't Ask Don't Tell—which does not allow openly gay, bisexual, or lesbian people to serve in United States military services—and became motivated to challenge their college's policy on same-sex relationships. Eric explained their approach:

We decided on National Coming Out day that enough was enough, and we were going to tell people. At this point we were so tired of hiding our relationship. We publicly came out to the entire university. We wrote a statement of what it is like to be gay at this college. We put our pictures on them and put them on the doors. The administration actually made us go talk to them... This was the point where the community found out we had gay people. We set up that night to have a vigil and did not know if people would really show up. Eighty-five people were there standing with us... The Dean of Students told us it was time for us to leave. They decide we can't stay there.

After leaving their religious institution they joined an activist group to travel around the country. Eric and his partner were disappointed they had to leave their institutions, but were ready to advocate for societal change. They joined a religious organization that was dedicated to actively challenging religious institutions that were against same-sex relationships. Eric explained more:

I was on this high of activism. It was a little crazy. But um, we withdrew and the director of the ride said, "Since you're not doing anything you should come with us." They were traveling on a bus around the country. I was like sure let's do this. That ride also helped me develop as well. I had newly came out and newly identified as a Christian who was gay, and a lot of the time I was around communities that were very different from what I was used to. I was at colleges that were just like minded and talking to people saying I am no different than you... It wasn't until that tour that I started calling myself a Christian again.

Eric faced the challenges within his relationship by actively seeking to change his institution as well as others around the country. He developed the skills to engage in critical dialogue about religion and sexuality, which also helped him overcome conflicts within his own identity. Eric recently published his stories about ex-gay therapy and being forced to leave his Christian college. Although Eric was still actively confronting the challenges of being a Christian in a same-sex relationship, he used his experiences to open dialogue on the complexities of multiple conflicting identities. The socialization he received came from a variety of sources during most of his life. As he began to deconstruct the messages about same-sex relationships he began to better accept himself. The process of accepting all of his identities collectively continued to develop as he also assisted others with developing all of their identities in a positive and healthy manner.

Chapter 5: Jenna, Supporting a Sorority Girl

Jenna was a confident senior at a liberal arts college outside of Los Angeles. As she entered her last semester of college she had an extensive resume of student leadership and organizing. Raised in a family that had both Catholics and Protestant Christians, Jenna was exposed to multiple aspects of the Christian faith, but identifies as Catholic. Although, Jenna had not actively participated with Catholic organizations while in college, it remained a part of her life. She began dating women her first year in college and during her sophomore year she began exploring the relationship between her sexuality and religion. Jenna described her experiences being involved in same-sex relationships as mostly positive and had learned greatly from them. Most of her challenges arose from the lack of support from her mom.

BACKGROUND: PARENTAL DISAPPOINTMENT

Jenna grew up in Southern California with a mother, father, sister, and a cousin who partially lived with her. Jenna was active in church as a youth with her family, but even from middle school she began to question the church's stances on abortion and sexual orientation. As she moved to college she had neither the desire nor the time to be active with any religious organizations. Jenna remembered her first attractions to women, and feeling dirty and shameful. She described her first recognition of this attraction:

I was just like sitting on the couch scrolling through the channels and I see the L Word and I was like 'What?' And I remember thinking like "Ya I shouldn't think that that's attractive or a turn on, but it is. What's wrong with me? Okay well maybe this is just like a dirty little secret because I have a boyfriend... Okay this is definitely new. I like this; this is attractive to me...But it's not supposed to be according to the church, according to the Bible. According to what's right." And then I would get a call that my boyfriend was outside... and we'd go off to the movies and life is all heterosexual and perfect like it's supposed to be.

Jenna's early attractions to women left her feeling as if something was wrong with her and she got these messages from her Church and its interpretation of the Bible.

During high school and into college Jenna began to separate from the church because she felt like they were hypocritical. There were messages preached about love and acceptance, but it was conditional. Jenna felt like they did not represent love, and began to reject organized religion. She disagreed with the ways in which the Catholic Church interpreted Bible passages, especially those on same-sex relationships and women. One instance in a church service the gospel made her uncomfortable and she felt condemned by the priest; it was always a struggle for her to attend Catholic Church services.

As Jenna moved to college and began exploring her sexual identity, she was scared to tell her parents she was a lesbian. It was terrifying for her to tell her family, mostly her mom because her mom had expected a particular heteronormative life for Jenna. Jenna knew her mom wanted her daughter to get married, have a traditional wedding and live as society expected young women to. Jenna's mom tried to understand and be supportive, but she did not know how to comfort or support Jenna during this time. Her mom did not use religion as a reasoning to be against Jenna being a lesbian, but it was just far from what her mom expected from her.

RELATIONSHIPS: LACK OF SUPPORT

Jenna began dating women her freshman year and had three significant dating-relationships while in college. Laura was her first girlfriend who was a former sorority sister that had graduated a few years before Jenna joined. Megan was in Jenna's pledge class and was a well-known lesbian activist on campus. Marissa was also her sorority sister, who was bisexual and eventually withdrew from the university to marry a man. Jenna had many break-ups and romantic upsets during her college years, and she often wanted support from her mom. However, the struggles in her romantic relationships often led to struggles with her mom.

As Jenna began dating Laura it helped her solidify and confirm her sexual identity. Jenna described her relationship with Laura as "feeling right and comfortable," but at other times it also felt like she was going crazy and was very uncomfortable having open dialogue about being with a woman. Jenna was conflicted as she wanted to discuss her attraction to a woman, but then was also afraid that her secret would be found out. There were also awkward feelings when Jenna brought her third girlfriend to Easter services. Jenna did not feel right sitting in church on a religious holiday next to her girlfriend.

Although Jenna's mom verbally expressed being supportive, her subtle messages and lack of interest made Jenna feel less accepted and not fully supported. Jenna's mom had created heteronormative expectations for Jenna, and when Jenna realized she was unable to meet those expectations she felt as if she was disappointing her mom. Jenna told about her mom's challenge:

My mom was the tougher one to crack 'cuz you know, you're parents grew up with the fairytale dream for your daughter and you know, Cinderella and the glass slipper and walking down the aisle in a white dress to not a groom, okay. That kinda blows up the fairytale dream that they had. It took my mom a while.

Jenna's mom made continuous efforts to grow more comfortable with Jenna dating women. Initially her mom would avoid talking about Jenna being with women; if Jenna brought up problems she needed advice on her mom would give cliché sayings while never acknowledging that the person Jenna was talking about was a woman. When Jenna told her mom she was in a relationship with a woman she decided not to bring her girlfriend home because she knew it would be hard for her mom. Jenna stated:

I took her (Megan's) best friend with me instead. But I didn't want my mom to feel like because of Megan's androgynous appearance to think, "Oh you're the girl that turned my daughter gay" because I knew that's how my mom would approach it.

Jenna's mom did not meet either of her first two girlfriends because she was concerned if her mom would approve of them.

As Jenna's three relationships went through challenges and eventually ended, her mom wanted to be there to support her, and Jenna wanted her mom to be able to support her as well. Jenna explained further:

I was frustrated. I was honestly like, "I want my Mom; I need my mom". You know, that's human nature. When you're faced with a threat you want your mom, and I wanted that support system. I wanted my mom to be there for me. I wanted my mom to agree with me. I wanted "Your child is always right, you stand by your kid no matter what they do"...She tried; like I could tell like behind it all that was you know the basis, but her generation like, it's different ideal and it took her a while. She couldn't just, the day after I come out, wave a flag and join PFLAG. My mom just didn't really understand the support that I needed to get that she wasn't really giving me at the time. And I understand that now, she's from a different era, a different time.

Jenna appreciated her mom's effort, but it was the subtle microaggressive words and behaviors and microinvalidations that hurt Jenna. Jenna's relationships seemed abnormal to her mother, so her mother was unable to help in a way that Jenna's mother would support if she was in a relationship with a man.

Jenna had another incident which brought more family conflicts. As she wanted to bring her girlfriend to Thanksgiving dinner at her aunt's house, but was pushed not to. Jenna described the conversation with her mom:

I had been talking to my mom… and she was like "You know you can probably still go to your aunt's… and I'm sure they wouldn't mind if you brought someone." I was telling my mom… "I'll probably want to take my girlfriend…" And she was like "Yea that'd be cool or I'm sure your aunt wouldn't mind if you brought a few friends. You can totally bring a couple of your sisters. I'm sure your aunt wouldn't mind". And I was like "Yea or I could bring my girlfriend…" And she was like, "Mmhmm, so did you hear that your sister and blah blah blah." So she still kind of avoids it…

Jenna later discussed how she wanted her mom to advocate for her to her conservative aunt, but was disappointed when her mom encouraged her to just bring other people instead to the Thanksgiving dinner.

The messages Jenna received from her mom were subtle, but affected how she managed her relationships and how accepted she felt within her families. Her family aimed to be supportive and welcoming, but often left her feeling isolated and distant from them. Jenna always felt like she grew up in a welcoming house and open church that taught love and acceptance, but the actions and attitudes she observed by her family and her church were different. She received messages that her relationships and her sexual orientation were not normal and not always welcomed

RESOLVING: FINDING SUPPORT AND POSITIVE AFFIRMATION

Jenna did not receive direct messages from her family that being in a same-sex relationship was forbidden and sinful. She did receive negative messages about same-sex relationships from her church; however, from a young age she tried to combat them. It was difficult for Jenna to not develop some ideology that being in a relationship was abnormal and wrong. Her early exposure to the *L Word* and the experience of bringing her girlfriend to church brought up feelings of shame, filth, and discomfort. Jenna stated that being at an open and diverse college assisted her greatly with feeling comfortable and exploring her religion and sexuality.

As Jenna began her first same-sex relationships her freshman year, religion was not a large part of her life, but it still affected her. Fortunately, Jenna had opportunities on campus to process how her religious and her sexual identities affected each other. Jenna's mentor invited her to attend a screening of *For* the *Bible Tells Me So* which had a profound impact on her. She explains further:

They had a screening of For the Bible Tells Me So *and...I went. I was supposed to go with my girlfriend at the time. And she wasn't there for some reason, and I just remember texting her throughout the entire thing, like "this is so powerful, this is inspiring" and it just started to get to me... That was the moment I think I really understood the diversity and acceptance at (my) college.*

54

Jenna also was able to watch another documentary, *Fish Out of Water,* which gave her a better understanding of Christianity and how people interpret the Bible. Jenna explains:

One of the professors who works in the religious studies department sent me an email about this, online lecture... And we sat through it and we listened to it together... It was all about this woman basically dissecting the Bible and it was amazing because she identified as lesbian and identified as religious and she went through, you know, all of the verses and all of the books and all of the chapters... But it was just amazing, like, people always want to bring out their own Bible quotes to support their points of view. But people don't realize that there are Bible quotes in there that can completely go against what you're trying to say. And it was really amazing.

Jenna was able to see how the documentary film maker was able to combine her religious and sexual identity in a healthy manner. Additionally, when she met Megan who was a confident lesbian in both queer communities and other parts of society, she was able to see positive examples of how people have reconciled multiple parts of their identity successfully. Seeing positive examples of non-heterosexual people made Jenna more secure in her sexual identity.

As Jenna faced challenges with her relationships she longed to have her mom support her through the emotional turmoil, but did not have that option. Jenna resolved her issue by finding other sources of support. One of the greatest supports to Jenna was her sorority. Jenna credits much of her ability to accept herself and her same-sex relationships to her sorority. She explained in the following words:

They're the ones that are with me everyday supporting me...1 told them and there was absolutely no judgment. And I actually credit a lot of my coming out, like 90% of my coming out, to my society. Because I had never been around a group of accepting people like that. And sexuality and sexual orientation was commonly spoken of and readily accepted and I wasn't used...

Jenna's sorority was one just one part of campus that made her feel welcomed. She often wondered what her life would have been like if she went to a different college. Jenna shared:

I think if I would have gone to another college which my mom was actually looking at a few very religious colleges for me to go to. Um, I just think about all the different ways my life would have gone. Like I probably would not have come out as early as I did if at all and if I did... but I would very possibly may have killed myself at an extremely religious institution that my parents well my mom, were looking at for me.

Jenna found many resources on her campus that helped her accept her sexuality and manage the conflicts within her relationships.

Jenna also used several other methods in order to cope with conflicts around her relationships and her sexuality. Writing was a tool Jenna used to manage her emotions. She would write to women she was in a relationship with as a way to communicate and she would also write to herself as way to express her emotions. Jenna also took time to get away from campus and spend time a places that brought her peace. When she was trying to make sense of conflict she would often find a place at the beach where she could reflect and process her thoughts and emotions.

The conflicts Jenna faced as she made sense of her religious and sexual identity brought about new purpose and confidence for her. As Jenna began to examine the oppression she felt from the church she turned to speak out to groups on campus. After watching the documentaries on campus she began sharing her stories on campus as an activist. As she brought awareness on the issues she faced within the church she felt like she helped her own self-confidence. Jenna's ability to reconcile her multiple identities brought about positive change on her campus and within herself.

Chapter 6: He Joonie, the Christian Oppressor

He Joonie was a senior Asian American Studies major at a California public university, and was a Korean-American queer identified female. He Joonie grew up highly involved with a Korean protestant church in Los Angeles, and she began challenging her church's authority as a high school student because she felt the effects of sexism and observed homophobia from the church and its leadership. While in college her relationships brought isolation from the queer community and the religious community. He Joonie's relationships often caused her to isolate herself and reject aspects of her identity in order to please others or hide from others. Through the struggles He Joonie faced, she was able to develop critical skills which led her to reconcile her identities and support others with similar life challenges.

Background: Always an Outsider

He Joonie grew up attending church several times a week and her dad was highly involved at their church. He Joonie's mom attended church, but placed education as a higher priority than religion, which He Joonie disagreed with and struggled to understand her mom's religious life. He Joonie saw the church as a patriarchal organization as a high school student and struggled to feel included as one of the few girls in the youth group. The teenage boys were often favored and she was excluded. He Joonie also witnessed her pastor publicly condemning one of her gay friends and banning him from the church. At the time He Joonie did not recognize her same-sex attractions, but she disagreed with the pastor and was unsure how to handle the situation. He Joonie enjoyed the spiritual and religious development she received from the church, but felt isolated and oppressed.

As He Joonie went to college she began exploring her sexuality with other women, but did not identify with a specific sexual identity. He Joonie did not give much thought to same-sex relationships, but always thought it was acceptable. He Joonie did not date men or women in high school because she grew up in a traditional Korean home where they were not allowed to date. He Joonie explained her first romantic interaction with another woman:

I didn't date being Korean, but I think the first encounter of a same sex like incident happened at the first party I went to in college. It was weird, but I was dancing with one of my friends who is a guy and somebody kinda like came from behind me and was caressing my body. It was a weird awkward moment... I guess it is different in feelings because, I guess it is not really fear, but it was uncomfortable.

He Joonie began to act upon her attractions to women, but it felt unnatural and awkward. Until this point in her life, everyone assumed He Joonie was heterosexual and the community at college was confused by her identity and actions.

RELATIONSHIP: FULFILLMENT AND ISOLATION

He Joonie met a woman at a party and it began as a casual interaction, but then evolved into a more substantial romantic relationship. As He Joonie began a relationship with a woman she felt it was a very positive part of her life. She described some of her initial feelings as she began her relationship with Cee (pseudonym):

Having somebody to talk to and be there with to hang out with. Always having somebody around, which is not something I normally like. I am normally a very independent person...I

would go out with her and we would go to the movies and have
dinner, cuddling. It was nice. Comforting having somebody there

He Joonie found it comforting to be in a relationship, and the person who she found compatible at the time was another woman. She described Cee as a person who was nurturing and comfortable to be with.

Cee was very active within the queer community on campus and was visible as a queer leader. As He Joonie began dating Cee it changed her perceived sexual identity, and many people questioned her place within the community. He Joonie described further:

I guess I have a hard time embracing queerness from this campus... they kind of force you to like really like write out your identities. Like when you apply for stuff, like they kind of force me and like when you write something they're like they always question it and it's just like I'm not down to have my identities questioned... Definitely I am a very private person, so the simpleness of it. Not that people don't know me, but people were all in the business. Some people found out and some people didn't. If somebody asked me I would tell them, but lots of people just assume. They assume you're straight or your identities for you. They do not allow for any clarifications.

He Joonie wanted to be a part of the queer community and be with Cee, but she felt pressured to pick a label to please other people. He Joonie and Cee later broke up and He Joonie was dating a man at the time she shared her story. She always felt she had to prove she still belonged in the queer community because she has a feminine gender expression and she also dated men.

As a Christian person in the queer community, He Joonie faced ridicule and isolation from members of that community. He Joonie shared:

A lot of my friends, including my closet friend, they are accepting me...but it's really not accepting me for (my) religion; is not really accepting me. So that's how friendships are broken, and I guess when I actively decided to pursue to God and really strengthen my relationship with Him, I lost a lot of friends...Enrique (one of her closest friends) really doesn't understand the religion in my life... He always says to me, "Your religious institute is what always oppresses me in society"... It's like you know people... in this community oppress the believers (Christians), they really do. Like a lot of them feel the need to really hide their religious beliefs.

He Joonie wanted to be an accepted part of the queer community but her religious identity was not accepted. She struggled to find friends in the queer community who were supportive of her religious identity as well. He Joonie refused to hide her religious life, which has caused her to lose a number of friends.

He Joonie also faced rejection from her Christian community. He Joonie was trying to reconcile her internal conflict with being in a same-sex relationship, but also faced condemnation from people at her church. He Joonie shared an incident about rejection she faced with a person from church:

One of the girls saw us kissing and it was very uncomfortable and I didn't go back to that church because that girl made me feel really uncomfortable. It was just like the dirty looks at first and then we had a talk and she told me I was going to burn in hell... I was condemned...That is when I learned verses like the man who shall not lie with another man. I got that from her. I read it in passing growing up during my youth days, but I never really reflected on it as much...She recited verses and told me that homosexuality is a sin and that I won't inherit the kingdom of God... You don't tell somebody they are going to burn in hell... I was in shock with her reaction.... I think after she said that to me I cried. Rephrase that, I did cry. I know the truth. I did cry.

He Joonie was hurt from the condemnation she received form a person representing the church, which caused her to struggle with her religious identity. He Joonie shared:

I guess that time period it pushed me away from God. It is like you expect God's people to be the most understanding and accepting and not as cliquish. You expect them to be more tolerant. Some people aren't. It kinda sucks... after that happened I just stopped going to the church and going to the Bible studies. I kinda fell off.
During the period He Joonie was away from the church she still identified as a Christian, but was sad she lost the spiritual support in her life due to her same-sex relationships.

Later that year He Joonie had an incident with some of her closest friends, which ended many of their friendships; she was hurt and isolated by them, so she turned back to God for support. As she began a new Bible study with a group of women from her church, He Joonie began to feel guilty about her relationship. The members of the Bible study were not supportive of her relationship whether it is with a man or a woman because they view it as a distraction from God. He Joonie continued to struggle with her relationship as she aimed to please God and enjoy a fulfilling romantic relationship. Even when He Joonie was in a relationship with men she faced similar doubts as she aimed to please God. She explained how she tried to balance her relationship with God and her relationship with a boyfriend or girlfriend. She shared:

God is a jealous God... I am not going to lie. He is jealous, but at the same time He is loving... I honestly think God wants me to be happy... It was really hard and we broke up like nine times. It all started with God because I wanted to be in the light and I didn't think I could have both, like be with him and be in the light. I thought I needed to give my whole life and make God my number one. In order to do that I need to X out everything else like school, work, friends, and make Him my number one priority. But I guess during that time period I was reading the Word and reflecting back on like, "I am really unhappy and depressed."

He Joonie struggled with all her relationships; she doubts if they are pleasing to God because her sexual activity made it difficult to feel like she is pleasing God. He Joonie described her doubts and recognized they were still present and on-going.

RESOLVING: FINDING INDIVIDUAL SUPPORT

As He Joonie faced challenges within the queer community and the Christian community she always felt like an outsider. The queer community wanted to force her to choose a specific sexual identity and condemned her for being Christian. The Christian community criticized her relationship with a woman and told her she was bound for hell. As He Joonie searched for a community where her entire identity could be supported, she felt disappointed by people. As she was searching for support she was also aiming to reconcile her feelings about being in a relationship and being sexually active.

One of the ways in which He Joonie began to make sense of her identities and her relationships was through a new understanding of reading the Bible. This began as a high school student when a female pastor visited and taught He Joonie about the story of the woman at the well. Through the story He Joonie learned much about the culture of the time it was written and the context of the passages. She began to have a more liberal understanding of the Bible and could see how it has evolved through time with different interpretations. He Joonie later read the Bible with a focus on God's plan for her life and grace. Another way in which He Joonie furthered her understanding of identity was through her academic work. She was able to take a number of courses which taught her critical thinking skills, and led her to further analyze her multiple identities.

After He Joonie faced condemnation from the church member she turned to activism as an outlet. She did feel lost at the time, but activism helped her make it through. He Joonie took the pain she received from the church and used it to try and make changes in society. She assisted in hosting a queer conference on campus, she planned lobbying trips to Washington D.C., and she planned workshops with the multicultural office. Part of the reason she got very active was to distract herself, but it aided her in making sense of her identities and also gave her space and time to process.

After some time He Joonie began to open up to other Christians about her sexual identity. She still faced some minor opposition, but she also found support from some Christians. As she was receiving opposition from one Christian friend about being on the campus pride committee, one of her Christian housemates was there to process the situation and was supportive of He Joonie's involvement with the queer community. He Joonie always viewed this friend as conservative and was surprised how supportive she was to her. As He Joonie faced numerous challenges in her life, she often turned to God as her ultimate support system. She learned that some communities will not support all of you and the challenges can be isolating. However, through developing a critical approach to identity, religion, and sexuality; finding a supportive friend, and relying on God she grew to be a support for other people struggling with similar conflicts.

CHAPTER 7: MARK, NOT IN MY DADDY'S CHURCH

Mark (a pseudonym provided by the participant) was a senior sociology major at a regional state university in the Midwest. He identified as multiracial, Black-American and White-American, and as a gay man. Mark grew up attending a Black church with his father, but recently had struggled to find a religious community where he felt welcomed. Mark worked in the campus LGBT office for over two years and viewed the LGBT community as his family. He strongly identified as a person with a disability, which he described as affecting his dating life. Mark was in a relationship for several years, but they rarely were able to be together in the same town. The relationship ended, and Mark wondered if he would ever be with someone again. Although Mark was an activist on campus he continued to struggle with accepting his sexual identity as he hoped to be free from "homosexuality" and possibly one day settle down with a wife and children.

BACKGROUND: FEARING THE LOSS

Both of Mark's parents were highly religious; his dad was a church leader and his mom was always very religious. Mark and his older sister were both baptized in his home church, which he also still called his "dad's church." Mark described his life purpose in trying to serve God and always wanting to be stronger in his faith. However, over the last decade his faith has been shaken by numerous circumstances. Mark's dad was the foundation of his faith, and when he was eleven years old his dad committed suicide. This tragic event caused Mark to question his faith. His dad was a church leader and the leader within his family's spiritual lives, which caused much confusion for Mark. Several years after his father's death he began exploring his sexuality, and the fear of rejection from his church family caused him to leave the church he called his home.

By the age of six Mark knew he was interested in the same-sex, but he was always told that his sexual identity was a choice; choosing to be with other men was wrong. As he later heard messages that affirmed his sexual orientation, Mark still struggled to believe that he was born with a gay identity. He shared, "It is something I did not believe and it is something I thought I shouldn't be this way. There was a point in time where I was told I was going to hell because of who you are. I didn't believe I was born this way." The guilt and struggles that Mark faced led him to seek out new perspectives from libraries and Internet resources, but his thoughts were in battle over his sexual orientation and destiny.

Through Mark's internal struggles he became fearful to remain connected to his Church. Since his father's death he viewed the Church as a symbolic representation of his father and his father's approval. Although Mark wanted to be connected to the Church he grew up in, if it were to outright reject and condemn him he would not be able to bare it. Mark longed to be part of his home church, but also any Black church. From his previous experiences he viewed the church to be condemning of his sexual identity, and he assumed they would ostracize and isolate him because of a same-sex attraction. Mark planned to find another church community that was more accepting of his sexuality but he held this church in a special place because it was the place where his deceased father was most actively engaged.

When Mark did begin to find a new church home he struggled to find a community that fully understood and supported him. The complications of being supported with sexual and religious identity are further compounded with those coming from racially marginalized groups. Churches in the United States are largely segregated based on race and ethnicity, and because he wanted to attend a Black church, he knew that he would likely not find one that also supported same-sex relationships. Mark's lack of religious and spiritual community led to a continued sense of isolation.

As Mark began to express to his family that he was not heterosexual he received mixed reactions. Mark was close to his older sister and looked to her as a mentor. She was one of the first people he told. Mark shared:

At first she was the one who was like, "No it is wrong. You are going to hell. You can contract AIDS through it." She was upset. She wanted me to go to counseling and she was not accepting... It was kind of hurtful. I thought she would be there for me. She came around afterwards. She got comfortable with the situation and everything. It was pretty hurtful sometimes. It was hard to see someone who you saw for so long and get close to turn and say "No it is wrong. I don't want you to be this way. I want you to change. I think it is a phase. I think you are going to get out of it." It was hard.

Mark faced direct rejection from his sister who was the key role model in his life. Mark feared rejection from his church, but he hid his sexual identity to avoid any condemnation. However, he did share his sexuality with his sister and his fears came to fruition. The few conversations he had with his sister had lasting impacts on his life-long struggles to accept his sexual orientation Mark highly-valued his sister's opinion and her views affected how he perceived himself. Eventually Mark's sister did become a strong support for him. She also later shared that she was also attracted to women, which created a unique bond between the two of them.

Mark later described his excitement for his gay identity and shared that his sexual identity was divine since he was born on National Coming Out Day. Mark felt like he was able to accept both his sexual and religious identities quickly, but he never fully believed that his identity was acceptable to God. Mark shared, "I do believe you can be gay and Christian, but a part of me just thinks hmm is this really true?" Mark often shared statements about his confidence and self-approval of his sexual identity and same-sex relationship, but he shared his insecurities and uncertainties about his sexual identity and religious identity. Mark was still attempting to make sense of his sexual identity and religious identity as he was finishing high and preparing to enter college. During the summer before Mark started college with is when he got asked out by his first boyfriend, Caleb (pseudonym).

RELATIONSHIP: LIVING IN DOUBT AND LONELINESS

During summer orientation Mark got a message on a social networking site from Caleb. Even as a high school student Mark never thought he would find someone because he had a disability so he was surprised that someone would be interested in him. Mark soon found out that Caleb also had a disability. Mark shared more about how their ability related to their romance:

He was also disabled himself, but his was more out there. It was more visible to see than my somewhat visible and invisible disabilities. Whereas I have to disclose my disability for people to know, they can see his. We just really connected. We had this bond. We knew a lot about each other. We dated for about two and a half years of and on.

Mark's relationship surprised him that he could find someone who could accept him for all of his identities. Although he was still attempting to resolve his feelings on his sexual orientation, he was joyful to find someone who he connected with.

Their relationship began just before Mark started college, and soon they were apart from each other. Mark would make many attempts to stay connected and visit, but the distance made a first and new relationship difficult. Over the next few years Mark and Caleb were able to sustain a relationship through multiple forms of communication. They faced numerous challenges, but they were still able to support one another in difficult times. Mark began to face intense challenges with his school, personal life, and health, which lead to what he calls his 'breakdown." Mark shared:

The breakdown was when I sort of isolated myself. I couldn't take care of myself as far as my health. I was not doing too well in school, grades were dropping. I didn't really have a social life So, what I did was end up in the hospital. Basically, he (Caleb) was there... He called me every day. He wanted to be there... He contacted my family. They were there... I do feel that God brought me through it and out of it because if it wasn't for my faith I would not have made it through that experience. If it wasn't for my Ex (Caleb) being there and supporting me as well as my family.

Mark's relationship with Caleb supported him through difficult times in his life, and stated that he will always be grateful to him.

Mark's family knew about Caleb and through his "breakdown" they could see that he was an asset to Mark's life, but they refused to talk about it or acknowledge the relationship he was in Over time his family began to acknowledge the relationship, and his sister later became a support system. However, early in the relationship Mark was not supported in his relationship with Caleb. Mark was excited to have a romantic relationship, but his family's lack of support was difficult. During the relationship Mark was not actively involved with his church. He would never expose his relationship to them because he would be unable to handle it if they rejected him. During this time Mark remained distant from his church and was fearful that they might find out he was in a relationship with Caleb.

After two and a half years of being in a shaky relationship, Mark and Caleb ended their relationship. The distance and expectations of being in a serious relationship while in college made it difficult to sustain a healthy relationship. The ending was not pleasant and Mark had many regrets. Mark shared:

I had a lot of regret. I felt really bad because of what happened. I sort of felt that I betrayed the person. I kind of felt the one that really loved me and was there for me. When I had a crises in 2008 I had a major emotional break down and he was there for me. Through it all, through thick and thin he was there for me. I still feel a little bit of regret. I still feel it hurt a lot of people including him. We have hurt each other a lot, but I still care for him and I hope he still feels the same.

Mark was unsure what he wanted out of the relationship, and he was unsure how to handle the ending of a relationship. The termination of the relationship was much more difficult for Caleb than it was for Mark, according to Mark. However, during this entire time, Mark still had many doubts about how God viewed him being in a relationship with another man. In addition to trying to manage his first same-sex relationship and make sense of his sexual and religious identities, he was also struggling to accept his identity as a multiracial man of color with a disability.

Mark was a campus activist, a staff member at the LGBT center, and was in a same-sex relationship for nearly three years; however, he struggled with doubt about his past relationship and any future relationship in which he might engage. Mark shared his ongoing doubts about his same-sex relationship:

I think that sometimes, "Am I going down the right path? Is this really what I want? Do I want to be gay all my life?" That is still a conflict I am dealing with trying to figure out what I want. "Is this really what God wants me to be? What if I could change this? Would I change it?" I don't know. I can't tell right now, but we will see what the future holds and if I end up getting married to a heterosexual partner. Maybe it will happen.

Mark openly shared his doubts and was honest about his desires to change his identities. He hoped that his sexual identity would change at some point in his life because he wanted to get married and have a "traditional" family. Mark shared:

I do think that maybe there is a possibility where I do have kids. I do believe that people's orientations change. I have a friend who was LGBT identified who got married and now is in a heterosexual relationship and has kids and is happy.

Mark worked to challenge society to accept people with same-sex attractions and relationships, but as he aimed to change societal norms he was also challenging his own doubts about being in a same-sex relationship.
Mark used his identity and relationship to educate others, but he shared that his life is challenging and he would not have chosen his identity. Mark shared more about his obstacles:

People think that being gay is peaches and cream and fine and dandy when it really is not. It is a challenge. Why would someone want to take a life where you are ostracized, that you get condemned and judged for who you are, and you get discriminated against? Why would someone choose that life? It is not easy. It is not easy going out each day and trying to figure out if I am going to be talked about. Am I going to be looked at because I am different because I am not with a person of the opposite sex? Those are things I think about...What if things were different? What if I wasn't this way? I am still doing a little bit of soul searching trying to find out in the next few years if I am going to be in another relationship with someone new or if I am going to be by my lonesome.

Mark was no longer in a relationship when he shared these thoughts. He mostly doubted his relationship because of societal treatment of people in same-sex relationships. Mark regularly struggled to be open about his same-sex relationship and was not sure if it was worth doing again. Mark described his ongoing inability to accept his sexual identity. Most of the time he felt comfortable and accepting of himself, but at times he battled negative feelings.

Mark was a Sociology major with a minor in women's studies and LGBT studies; therefore, he was well aware of how his self-perception was constructed. Even knowing multiple perspectives on sexuality and socialization, Mark struggled to accept himself. Mark explained where he thought his negative ideas came from:

It comes from my environment I am in. The people I am around who constantly use the Bible to condemn and the church to condemn and use the passages to condemn homosexuals um. It's just my thoughts I have. I don't think of it every day; some days I don't... It depends on what is going on that day and the situation I am put in. If I am at church I think about it. If I am in a worship service I think about it. If I am watching a choir or hear gospel music I think about it. I think it is those daily encounters with the church or anything spiritual or worship related makes me think, "Am I supposed to be gay?"

Although Mark knew what he thought and felt about himself was inaccurate and detrimental, he continued to struggle to overcome negative ideas about their same-sex relationships and sexual identity. Mark recognized his identity acceptance process was on-going and with time he hoped to construct more positive image of himself.

The struggle to fit his sexual identity and religious identity was on-going for Mark. Mark questioned his spiritual growth and thought it might be lacking because of his sexuality. He has wanted to pray in tongues for many years, but it not happened yet. As he questioned why this might be he shared, "I feel that I am still balancing that and growing in my faith and figuring out if me being gay is the right thing. Something, maybe me being this way, is a conflict keeping that from happening (speaking in tongues)." Mark's doubts were not always present, and they were very situational. Mark knew when he was more likely to question his sexuality. When thinking about when and why he questioned his sexuality he shared:

I don't think of it (sexuality being wrong) everyday. Some days I do, some days I don't. It depends on what is going on that day and the situation I am put in. If I am at church I think about it. If I am in a worship service I think about it. If I am watching a choir or hear gospel music I think about it. I think it is those daily encounters with the church or anything spiritual or worship related makes me think, "Am I supposed to be gay."

Mark still associated anything Christian or religious to being anti-LGBT. For many years he viewed the Christian faith as an institution that rejected him and his sexuality. Mark also, shared that he felt isolated at times even within LGBT community spaces. His religious identity was constantly questioned. Mark shared, "People always ask you, 'Can you really be gay and Christian.' Yeah, you can be. That is a problem I get all the time. Mark did not feel like he found a place that fully supported his sexual and religious identity.

Although mark had been single since ending his relationship with Caleb, he did long to be with someone again soon. His fears of being alone resurfaced after he and Caleb were over. Since they ended Mark has struggled with loneliness and fear. He shared:

I never really had anything else (relationships). I never got any other offers. I didn't have many options open. I never experienced any relationship after that. Hopefully after I graduate or later on in life somebody will catch my eye or I will catch their eye and hopefully we will get together.

Mark has specific things he hopes for and one of which was a sense of spirituality. Mark shared:

Things I would look for is first and foremost is that they have a faith in God first and foremost. They don't necessarily have to be strong in their faith, but they have to at least know basically whether they have faith.... I think it is important to be strong in your faith...

Having faith was important to Mark, which was one of the reasons it was hard for him to find someone to be in a relationship with. Mark did not want to be alone, but did not want to settle. As a gay man on a college campus he struggled to know who was an option to date. Mark shared:

With being gay, one challenge is we all want to be loved and we want to find someone to share our lives with. We don't want to be single all our lives. We want to be able to share our physical aspects as well as well as the intimate things... I want that in life. For gay people I think it is harder. Certain people are still in the closet and hiding who they are. You really don't know who is gay out there.... That is a challenge for me. I want that so bad. I want that so much. I know that if God wanted that for me he would make it happen. It's scary because nobody wants to be alone there whole life and not getting married and sharing their life with somebody. Temptation is a challenge. Being tempted to date anybody and being with anybody you want. I don't want to be alone.

Mark struggled with loneliness and fear of never finding another relationship in addition to trying to gain support from his family and religious community. Mark's struggles led him to seek a community where his sexuality could be accepted and he could educate others.

RESOLVING: ON-GOING ACTIVISM

Through Marks many struggles he found resources that helped him make sense of his internal conflicts as well as find community. Marks's struggles largely focused on an internal battle with his thoughts. He aimed to further understand his prior socialization and then find alternatives to expand on those perspectives. The Bible had been used to make him feel that he was unacceptable to God. He began to gain a new understanding of reading the Bible. Mark shared:

Because the black church condemns, ostracizes, judges, points fingers; they use the Bible as a tool to condemn homosexuality. First and foremost we all have different interpretations of the Bible. I have my own interpretation of the Bible as well as someone else may have their own interpretation of the Bible...I don't think people should judge other people by what the Bible says because there are certain passages in the Bible that say you should do certain things, but people are still doing them regardless of what people say. It is sort of just a foundation.

Once Mark began to understand how the Bible can be interpreted in multiple ways and used in a variety of cultural contexts he was better able to accept himself. Mark also received counseling services for much of his life, which he found beneficial. Seeing a counselor regularly allowed him to talk about issues that were locked inside. Mark's counselor helped him see the big picture with his internalized homophobia; he struggled to want to change from being gay. Regular counseling helped him stop trying to change his sexual orientation.

Mark also gained a great deal of self-acceptance when individuals in his life affirmed his sexual and spiritual identities. Mark stated, "I talked to certain people. I confided in certain people and they told me, 'You're not going to hell because of who you are. It is ok for you to be this way. It is OK to be gay.'" Mark's mom eventually became one of his most significant supporters. Mark shared:

My mom was the person first and foremost who believed that being gay was not a sin or me being attracted to the same sex is not wrong because the day she found out that I was gay she came to me and said, "Mark, I love you. I love you for who you are. If you want to cross dress, dress in drag, or whatever I still love you no matter what." From that point in my life I knew that nobody else in the world mattered.

Mark's mom's support fluctuated, but her verbal confirmation of this sexual orientation allowed him to further accept himself. Mark also had a friend who was heterosexual, who he calls his straight ally, also supported and would talk with him through challenges.

Mark found several heterosexual individuals in his who affirmed his sexual orientation, but he still longed for a community. Mark found community through involvement in the LGBT student organization and LGBT center on campus. Mark stated, "I was able to find that support group and that place of comfort that place of belonging to be open about myself and who I am and to grow as a person..." Mark was looking for a place where his sexual orientation was validated and normalized. He found that within LGBT student organizations. Mark shared:

I think seeing and meeting other LGBT identified folks helped me come to terms with my identity. After doing my own research; doing my own readings; getting to know other people; seeing

*people like me portrayed on television and media and news
really helped me with my identity.*

Mark finally found a community when he got to college through
getting involved with the LGBT student organization. The
LGBT community allowed him to feel included and not feel
abnormal. Mark also gained this feeling when he began watching
television programs and movies which featured LGBT characters
in a positive portrayal. Additionally, Mark received critical support from administrators at his university.

Mark became very involved with the LGBT center at his
university during his freshman year. He eventually received a
paid position in the center. The LGBT center had a full-time
administrator who changed Mark's life and helped him become
the activist he now is. Mark shared:

*My boss was one of those people who were stood close by me
and really helped me wrap my head around the whole gay thing.
She has helped me understand it is ok to be this way. You are
who you are. It is ok to be who you are. She was my support
system. She was like the mom I never had. She would talk to me
and support me with anything going on as far as emotional or
academics or studying. She would all ways have an open door
policy where she was able to talk to me. I think she was one of
the persons who really encouraged me to go out there and share
my story and be visible and tell other people what it means to be
gay; to go out there and talk to other people; to find a church
home where I feel comfortable with that I feel ok with... She was
one of those upfront people that I really admired.*

Mark's involvement in the university LGBT center allowed him
to gain support from a student affairs professional, who was an
expert in LGBT identity development, as well as gain a better
understanding of his purpose in life. Mark began to enjoy his job
and feel like he had a place to each day and make a difference.

Mark's student position became more than just a financial resource. Mark shared, "I like what I do. I know that I am happy to go work each day and that I am making a difference in the school community and the LGBT community and just educating others about LGBT identity." Prior to becoming a paid staff member Mark had also volunteered as on a speaking panel telling his story about "coming-out."

Through Mark's personal struggles and support he received from educators, he knew he wanted to continue working in a helping profession or social services after graduating. Mark had become well aware of his multiple identities and how they fit within society. Mark shared:

That is one thing that being multiracial, being LGBT, being in same-sex relationships, being a person of color for that matter it really shows that you know who you are and you know what other people experience. You have really an advantage in life, but you also have privileges as well as oppression.

As Mark became more aware of his identities he became more focused on advocating for social justice. His activism expanded to include those with similar and different identities as his own.

Through all of Mark's struggles he had many great resources to support him and assist him on his journey of self-acceptance. However, the one thing that he attributes his resilience and survival too is his faith. Mark encountered many obstacles, but he says his faith is what helped him make it through. Although he did at times rely on family and friends, those support systems were inconsistent. Mark stated, "Not my family and not my friends, not my social outlet, but my faith has been there. Believing in something. Believing in a high power, something I will always have." Through Mark's conflicts he has questioned his faith, but with the trials it grew to be a central part of his life. He aims to use his life experiences to passionately serve others.

CHAPTER 8: DONALD, NOBODY HATES ME LIKE ME

*D*onald (a pseudonym provided by the participant) graduated from a Christian university within the last year and has spent his time processing the end of his last relationship. Donald spoke of his same-sex relationship through the perspectives and experiences of a Christian man who is deeply committed to social justice; some of this he attributed to being a person of color and a sexual minority. Donald was born in Hawaii, lived in a variety of places throughout the United States, and went to a college in Southern California. Donald grew up with Christian parents and identified as multiracial. As Donald discussed his past relationship, feelings of guilt, shame, and self-hatred were still fresh; moreover, he hesitantly shared that his relationship ended due to his infidelity. His boyfriend was the one place he found community, and now he was actively searching to find a place that supported his religious and sexual identity.

BACKGROUND: FEARING WHO YOU ARE

Prior to engaging in a relationship, Donald's identity was feared, hidden, and marginalized. Donald's family was Christian, but he heard little about gay people or same-sex relationships from them. Donald learned from his church and from other subtle messages that being with the same-sex was wrong, and these beliefs stirred a constant fear in him. As Donald realized he was attracted to men he feared that this attraction would lead him to identify as gay. Donald wanted to talk about his challenges, but he was terrified for anyone to know about his attractions. Donald shared his fear:

Growing up I thought it was wrong and I would try to hide it. It was my worst fear. Then once I finally realized that after twenty years that the attraction was not going away. It was becoming bigger and bigger for me... I was at the point in my life where I thought if I could pray for myself to change because for me knowing that I had this attraction to men, my biggest fear was growing up to be gay.

After years of prayer and pleading to change, Donald chose to go to a Christian college with an honor code prohibiting same-sex relationships as a way to keep him from engaging in same-sex relationships. As Donald dealt with his sexual identity he felt no community support or inclusion and had to hide his same-sex attractions. Donald stated, "There was none (community). I had friends, but during the coming out process I had none (community)." If Donald engaged in a same-sex relationship he would be expelled from the university, so he was fearful to expose his same-sex attractions. After Donald's first physical interaction with a man he was traumatized and cried for three days; moreover, he did not know what to do and because he was at a Christian university he thought he could not talk to anybody. Donald's isolation and fear led him into depression. He explained further:

My first semester at (college) was very depressing because I felt very by myself... It was more of a sense to scare myself or scare the gay out of me, but I tried to overdose... I don't want to say I couldn't handle it anymore, but I didn't want to. I was just exhausted...I knew the amount of pills I took wouldn't do it. I attempted, but it was more self-punishment...I think part of me just wanted, I knew I wouldn't say anything, but I wondered if anyone cared enough to notice...I remember having a picture of my nephew by my desk and...I remember looking at that picture and bawling my eyes out acting like I was talking to him and just saying "I can't do this anymore," and then convincing myself that he would be better off without me because I was gay. I remember those words coming out of my mouth and how bad of an example I would set for him.

Throughout Donald's interviews he spoke of his nephew and was deeply concerned for his wellbeing. Donald wanted only the best for his nephew and feared that his sexual identity would hinder him from being a good uncle. During previous times that he had suicidal thoughts he avoided acting on them because of thoughts of his nephew, but during the incident he described he was overwhelmed and just wanted to end his life. After Donald woke up the next day he somehow felt better about his situation and identity. He decided his same-sex desires were not going to change and he wanted to embrace his sexual identity.

As Donald began identifying as gay, he struggled with his religious identity; he always felt that you could not be gay and Christian at the same time. He remembered learning from the church that if you were gay then you were not going to heaven. Donald only remembered a few gay people when he was younger, and he perceived them negatively because he saw them as rebellious and anti-Christian. Donald stated:

The only gay guys I knew or had met, were very flamboyant and very effeminate and had tremendously rebelled against anything they had been brought up by...At that point in time, it was very much, the way I saw my Christian friends looked at him. They did not approve. Those were the examples that I knew. I did not know any more masculine gay guys. I did not have any examples. To be gay meant to be like that, and none of them were Christian In my mind it came down to being gay or being Christian. There did not seem to be room for both.

Donald viewed gay men as rebellious, anti-Christian, and associated with femininity; moreover, Donald viewed feminine men in a negative manner. Donald's gender expression was mostly masculine, which also caused some confusion for him because he struggled to see a gay identity separated from femininity. As Donald tried to make sense of his religious identity and sexuality he turned to online communities, which he often felt put his sexual health in risky situations. After a variety of emotionless, physical sexual interactions, he found a more supportive online community, which is where he met his boyfriend, Kyle (pseudonym).

RELATIONSHIP: DEVELOPING IDENTITY WITHIN A RELATIONSHIP

Donald was searching for a community and his only source was online since he was at a Christian university prohibiting same-sex relationships. Donald's campus was also located too far from a metropolitan gay community for him to engage with. Donald found Kyle and their online meeting quickly turned into Donald's first relationship. The relationship confirmed Donald's identity and fulfilled something he felt like he had always been missing. Donald was excited because he found someone who wanted to be with him, and this person was a gay Christian. Donald shared:

My feelings were ecstatic and overjoyed because I had finally met someone that I identified with and who identified with me... Joyful like no other. Happy. Not really hesitant. It was a sense of finally. Finally feeling like I could be myself more. Looking back I was not myself.

As Donald reflected back on the relationship he felt like he was not ready for a relationship. One of the biggest conflicts was related to Donald trying to figure out how his multiple identities could exist within him.

When Donald began the relationship with Kyle he was very vulnerable and did not know who he was. Donald explained more about the multiple dimensions of their relationship:

I was really young and he was the first one I loved. But at that point and time I wanted a friend I could talk to. That's what he

became, my best friend... I'm glad it was with him that, but I
wish we had met after I let myself do the processing and
individual identity and understanding. I didn't know myself. I
didn't know anything.

Kyle helped Donald process his religious and sexual identity, but
it also caused many strains on their relationship. Donald was
longing for a community, and when he met Kyle he became
Donald's entire community. Kyle identified as Christian and
helped Donald see it was possible for both of these identities to
coexist. Through their relationship Donald was able to
strengthen his religious identity. God came first in both of their
lives. They went to church together and were able to have
conversations about religion and spirituality. Donald also said
his religious life became better while in a relationship because he
was happier. Donald viewed Kyle as his community that fully
embraced his sexual and religious identities. It became problem-
atic because Kyle was Donald's only community and when their
relationship ended Donald struggled to cope. He feared he would
be alone forever and he had no community that could support his
religious and sexual identities.

Another conflict that Donald faced within his relationship was
being forced to hide his relationship at his college and live in
fear of being discovered. A few months into Donald's relationship he was investigated by the associate dean regarding his
relationship with Kyle. Donald explained the conflict further:

I was still at a private Christian university; I was aware of the
trouble I could get into once I started dating and that was what I
was confronted with down the road. Six months later from when
I started dating I was called out about it by an associate dean
and I had four months left of school, and they told me to make a
choice. At the time I wish I could have told them go screw
themselves... For two months I lived that little bit of a lie.

Donald lived in fear that he would be found out and created lies about where he was going each weekend in order to be with Kyle Although he wanted to be honest and true to his relationship and identity, he knew he would risk getting expelled. As Donald faced challenges with his relationship he struggled to find people and a community to turn to for support.

Donald's relationship ended due to him cheating, and he dealt with extreme guilt and shame. He also had to cope with a break-up with little support and the fear of it being exposed at his college. Donald felt terrible about himself and it took a long time to forgive himself; he hated himself and was angry with himself. As Donald dealt with emotional conflict he struggled to find a place that could support him. Donald longed for a community that could support his religious and sexual identities. As the relationship ended, Donald struggled with feelings that he would be alone for the rest of his life. He wanted his future partner to be spiritually supportive, and he felt like that would be hard to find within gay communities.

RESOLVING: FINDING A COMMUNITY

As Donald faced challenges with his sexuality and religion, he sought out resources actively, but those resources were not on campus since he was at an institution that prohibited same-sex relationships. Donald did find some support in online communities; however, he found many negative sites before finding a place that was able to provide positive resources. Much of Donald's reconciliation between his religious and sexual identity came through his relationship with Kyle. Kyle was a positive example of a gay Christian and allowed Donald to express his concerns out loud with someone who understood.

As Donald began his relationship, he relied on Kyle to assist him with making sense of his identities. He explained:

It was still a very confused state. Once I or my quote unquote coming process moved into a process it was just weird that I became comfortable in my own skin, with who I was, with who I always feared I was. My ex had a lot to say and hearing what his experiences were had tremendous effects on how I viewed the possibility of being gay and Christian. It was still a hard long process trying to figure out what that meant for me. Once I started talking to my friends and hearing the research they had done and different things and that historically some of the passages have referred to actually this or that and I started to look into it more myself. I started to get a better grasp of what it meant for me and how I felt OK now. Yeah, I became very comfortable very quickly. I eliminated a lot of a process of what it normally would be.

Once Donald was able to understand different interpretations of the Bible given the historical and cultural contexts, he was able to have a better grasp on his identities. Donald began to critically examine much of what he was taught and believed. His self-acceptance took much time and effort, but hearing from multiple supportive people aided him on his journey.

Much of Donald's relationship problems stemmed from him trying to figure out who he was during this process. After the relationship ended he fell into a depression. Donald turned to therapy to assist him in making sense of this challenge within his life. He wanted to go to therapy for some time, but the break-up pushed him to find someone to assist him with his mental, emotional, and spiritual well-being. Donald felt like he had someone who could focus on him and his feelings and he could let out all of his emotions and anguish without facing any bias or judgment, which assisted him in processing personal and rela-tionship issues. As Donald searched for a therapist he aimed to find someone who would understand his sexual and religious identities. The therapist he chose received her degree from the same religious institution he was attending, which caused hesitations. However, he was able to process his relationship with her without fear or judgment and greatly benefited from her services.

As Donald faced challenges finding community at his institution, he decided to open up to some friends. Donald was surprised by his friends' positive reactions, and he quickly built a network of supportive people. Although they were not part of a gay or queer community, they tried to support him and did not give him negative feedback. Donald explained how his friend supported him during his break-up:

My best friend, she was just there for me. Even if it was just sitting there watching a movie or both of us doing homework and not talking, but having her there and knowing that she was there was huge because it allowed me to not be alone during that period. I don't have family that lives in the area, but she was my family.

In addition to having supportive friends on his campus he also found a mentor from his job in a student affairs office that was able to provide support. Donald shared:

My mentor at the time of course was another who I would meet with me at least once a week in addition to going to therapy to just update her on the process because she was someone I respected and someone who could give advice and criticism and I would take it wholeheartedly.

Donald did find a support network on campus, but he longed for a spiritual community. As his relationship ended and he was struggling emotionally, he went to church.

Donald wanted to change a lot of things about himself and he viewed the church as a place of spiritual support. He did find a church that openly supported same-sex relationships and he described it with these words, "The church and what they teach provides me with the food I need and aligns with what my faith needs are." Donald struggled to find a true community at the church, but it was a place he felt welcomed and accepted.

As Donald faced challenges reconciling his religious and spiritual life he forced himself to process the conflicts he encountered. He avoided neglecting the issues and tried to actively process and resolve them. Through the trials he faced, Donald knew his faith and spiritual life grew. His sexual identity was attributed to his growth in many parts of his life including his faith. Donald examined who God was and what religion was, and knew his religion is personal to him. Donald knew he would face other major challenges in his life and the process he had endured would aid him as he encounters future life trials.

CHAPTER 9: VALERIE, HIDE IT IN THE HOOD

Valerie (a pseudonym provided by the participant) was a junior environmental science major at a California public university and was seen as one of the most active queer student leaders on campus. She was a Latina queer identified woman who avoided labeling herself as lesbian or bisexual. Valerie grew up with an extremely religious mom and a supportive dad who divorced when she was a toddler, so she spent time living between both households. Valerie claimed a queer identity in high school, and her twin sister also identified as queer. The two of them took their ridicule and turned it into active organizing for the queer community, which resulted in them establishing a gay straight alliance at their high school. Valerie grew up in a mostly Latino neighborhood in Southern California, and often feared for her safety because of her sexual identity and gender expression. Although Valerie was an active student leader within queer communities in high school and college, she hid her sexual identity and relationship from some people, including her mom. Valerie's former girlfriend, Samantha (pseudonym), did not claim any type of queer or non-heterosexual identity, and also hid her relationship from her parents.

BACKGROUND: CONDEMNING GENDER EXPRESSION AND SEXUAL IDENTITY

Valerie learned from an early age that being with another woman was unacceptable to society and to her mom. Her socialization on gender expression and sexual identity later affected her self-identity, religion, and relationship with her girlfriend. Valerie did not agree with her mom at the time of the interview, but she still did not want to lose their relationship. The messages Valerie received came from a variety of sources, although most of the negative messages she recalls came from her mom. She remembered in middle school telling another girl that she liked her, but the girl told her that it was wrong. This incident was one of the first messages Valerie remembered receiving that made her feel negative about her sexuality and forced her to learn that it was socially unacceptable to like girls; from that point onward she tried to hide her sexual attraction to other women and girls.

Valerie internalized the messages she received and struggled to define her sexual identity. She shared:

There was one time when I had those internal struggles "Oh I shouldn't be doing this. I need to find help and someone to convince me it's not okay, so I can have reason to stray away from it." But at the same time I could never do that 'cuz that's just who I am and I've accepted it.

These internal struggles also affected her religious life. Valerie shared some of her early struggles:

When I was younger I definitely thought that God hated people, I mean gay people. And if I ever came out as gay, then things in my life were gonna go completely bad because of it, and that it would be all God telling me yeah you shouldn't be gay. And here's what happens to gay people when they come out.

Valerie wanted her same-sex desires to go away, but she was unable to suppress the emotions. As she began to accept her attraction to other girls, she struggled to understand how it would fit with her religious identity.

Valerie could not comprehend what it meant to be queer and Christian. People told her that she could not be Christian and queer. She felt like she was always being judged within the queer community, so she avoided talking about her religion in queer spaces. Valerie also felt like people thought she was a hypocrite because she identified as Christian, but was still involved with women. Valerie shared:

There was an internal struggle I felt that I couldn't be religious and queer because it was just wrong and it was very contradicting of one another. I felt like, "OK you can't have a relationship with God or that faith if you are queer."

She had not seen these two identities present in someone before, and she questioned if she could reconcile these parts of her life. Valerie also worried that the queer community would think that she only went to church or claimed a Christian identity in order to redeem her for her same-sex relationship. Valerie struggled with how she thought God viewed her same-sex relationship as well as how the church and the queer community would perceive her.

As Valerie received negative reactions from society, she and her sister used the challenges to motivate them to makes changes. They started a gay straight alliance at their high school, which brought on additional criticism from teachers, parents, and other students. Although she and her sister were both actively confronting oppression in their school, neither of them could confront their mom. Valerie constantly received negative words about her gender expression and about queer people from her mom. Valerie was a masculine woman and her mom pushed strict traditional gender roles onto her. Her dad would let her wear what she wanted, which was clothes deemed more suitable for boys. However, when she went to her mom's house to visit she would want her to wear a dress. Valerie shared more:

But whenever we would visit her, it was always very scary for me...With that came like the criticism. "Why don't you girls wear dresses and fix your hair and your father's not doing a good job raising you girls. People are not going to like you if you don't dress a certain way and they're gonna look down on you." That was like I don't know, very discouraging sort of and made me just not want to go visit my mom at all because I guess she instilled this fear in me. Or if I didn't meet certain standards, I'd feel bad about myself.

Valerie's mom associated masculine women with queerness, so she disapproved of Valerie's masculine gender expression. Even if Valerie was not in same-sex relationships, she worried about her masculinity. Valerie shared this story:

We would see not even a gay couple on the street, but a female who happened to look like she was a lesbian or had more masculine attributes to herself; she would always try to get it across my head "See that, that's a perfect example of how you shouldn't live your life. You shouldn't go out there liking other women because people are gonna look down on you and no one's gonna you know, really like support you and it's just you know something that God doesn't want for you and you're supposed to be with man and have a family." So like hearing that, it just made me think, maybe she does have a point as far as making her happy as well maybe I shouldn't be doing this or even thinking about stuff like this. I should be focusing solely on school and trying to see more religious outlets; like start going to church again and stick with that, so that I won't have these thoughts.

As Valerie left for college the thoughts she had formed from her mom's words were not easy to overcome. Valerie was active in a queer community at her school, but she still was unsure if her sexuality was acceptable to God. Valerie felt that she had to hide her sexuality and same-sex relationship from her mother and others who might share her secret to her mother. She questioned her attraction to women, her religious identity, and her gender expression.

91

RELATIONSHIP: LIVING IN FEAR OF BEING FOUND OUT

As Valerie began her first relationship with Samantha she was still struggling to make sense of her religious and sexual identities. Samantha and Valerie were friends at first and then they became romantically involved; however, Samantha did not identify as queer or any non-heterosexual identity. Samantha told Valerie that after they broke up she would probably never date another woman. As Valerie began her relationship she was very uncomfortable and had many doubts about whether it was appropriate. Valerie explained:

My previous relationship was very difficult for me to be sort of be comfortable in my own skin because I was always thinking about like "What, well should I really be doing this? Or is this just a phase for me? Because you're a woman and you're supposed to bear children and be with a man and all this stuff" And then I started questioning it too, "Oh would I actually be happy with a woman or with a man?"

Valerie knew she was attracted to girls and women for over a decade, but as she began a relationship she had to reevaluate the conflicts surrounding her sexuality and religion. The mix of emotions confused her. At one point she was excited to have someone and it felt natural, but at another point she felt uncomfortable, unnatural, and fearful that her mother would find out.

Valerie's and Samantha's relationship often revolved around them trying to hide their relationship from their families. Their inability to be open caused strains on their relationship and eventually resulted in them ending their relationship with each other. Both Valerie and Samantha were concerned about their moms knowing about their relationship. Valerie hid the relationship from her mom because she was scared that her mom would condemn her to hell if she found out. Valerie's mom told her she would be embarrassed if her daughter was not heterosexual. Valerie shared:

I would focus on what she was saying about them being gay and going to hell and if any of her children were to be gay she would be totally embarrassed and you know wouldn't know what to do with herself, and it would be embarrassing for herself if anyone else found out. That for me was when it became more like insecure about coming out or being OK with who I was. Well, I was like "My mom doesn't approve of it then I can't be OK with it either." Her word means everything to me. I didn't get the vibe or stigma from society. It was mostly driven by my mom... she is not going to be OK with it and telling me all this and that is her saying, "If you come out I am going to disown you and not approve of it. My love for you is going to change."

Valerie feared that her relationship would disappoint her mom and shame their family, so she chose to hide it from her mom. Although she disagreed with her mom, she still did not want to lose that relationship. During this part of the interview, Valerie put all of the blame for her negative ideas and internal homophobia on her mom as she claimed she never got negative vibes or messages from society. However, at other times during the interviews Valerie discussed how classmates, neighbors, and teachers all told her that her sexuality and same-sex relationships were wrong.

Valerie had a complex relationship with her siblings; at times she needed them for support, but at other times she feared disclosing her relationship to them. Her brothers had used her secret as a way to blackmail her. If they needed something from her they would threaten to tell their mom about her relationship with Samantha. Not only did Valerie hide her relationship from her family, but she also hid her queer activism from her mom. Her mom knew that she was very active on campus, but she did not know what issues she was advocating for. Valerie had to hide many aspects of her life, in order to maintain some type of relationship with her mom. She shared:

I wish she could be more involved because the main thing is that she doesn't know me enough. I am her daughter. She doesn't know enough about me to know where I am coming from. It is hard to talk to her about a lot of things...

Valerie loved her mom and wanted a close and healthy relationship with her, but due to her mom's negative views on her sexuality, Valerie hid large parts of her life from her mom. Valerie often wanted someone to talk to, but felt like she had no one she could share these parts of her life with.

Samantha also hid their relationship from her family, but her mom did find out which caused many complications in their relationship and eventually led to its demise. As Samantha's mom began to speculate that they were in a romantic relationship Valerie began to feel hatred from Samantha's mom. Samantha's mom did all she could to try to separate them. Valerie explained the incident:

I was like "Here I go again because someone I really want to be with, but I can't be with her because someone disapproves of it." Her being her mom, and my thing also was I was a little scared because I was like "Oh what if my mom finds out?" It wouldn't be like me telling her, it'd be someone else; "Hey did you know your daughter's like a lesbian" or whatever... That sort of brought that sentiment from like a lot when I was younger or when I was like "Wait, should I be doing this?"

The stress of hiding their relationship was part of the reason that Valerie and Samantha ended their relationship. Valerie and Samantha faced opposition from many sources, but their families made it challenging to engage in a healthy relationship.

RESOLVING: SEEKING OUT DIVERSE PERSPECTIVES

As Valerie faced numerous conflicts interpersonally as well as in her relationship, she found numerous ways to resolve them and cope through stressful situations. As Valerie tried to make sense of her understanding of her religious and sexual identities, she had to examine the messages around her and then seek out differing perspectives on queer people and same-sex relationships. Valerie examined religion and how it related to social constructs within her identity. She also began to examine her identity within the perspective of other religions. As Valerie realized that her religious organizations would likely not accept her, she began to focus on how she could accept herself outside of other organizations' acceptance of her. Valerie also adjusted the way in which she read the Bible; instead of looking at the text as exact, specific truth she began to read it to understand the morals and their application within her life.

Valerie also changed her views as she met other queer people who were also religious. Valerie shared:

I think it changed over time just by seeing not just me by myself, but I came across a lot of people that were religious and I had no idea they were gay. And they were telling me "Yeah I have a partner of the same sex. And we live together," and I was like "Really? How do you yourself deal with that?" And they would tell me "Yeah you know, it's difficult to deal with certain people. But when it comes to God, He's gonna love you no matter what."

Meeting people who had reconciled their identities gave Valerie hope that she could also make sense of her religious and sexual identities. Positive examples expanded her understanding of queerness, and helped her visualize the complexity of identities. While on campus she often faced challenges about being religious within a queer community; therefore, she sought out other religious queers and they were able to support each other.

Many people assumed she was a certain way because she identified as Christian, so eventually she stopped talking about her religious identity unless someone asked her.

Valerie turned much of her opposition into activism. As she transitioned from high school to college, she was hesitant to get heavily involved in the queer community. However, Valerie met people who encouraged her to get involved with political campaigning and then other forms of campus activism. As Valerie began to get more involved with campus organizations she became more comfortable with herself. Valerie also shared, "They (activist organizations) sort of came up out of necessity not really because I always wanted to be an activist. I never really saw myself getting active in the gay community." Valerie wanted to do something with the feelings she was having because of oppression, and student activist organizations helped her develop confidence, a sense of identity, and her leadership skills.

As Valerie faced challenges with her mom and her relationship with Samantha, she did have support. Although Valerie and her twin sister faced some conflicts, they were supportive of one another. Her twin is also queer, so they had an understanding of each other's challenges and could truly understand the other. After Valerie had negative experiences with her mom, she would talk to her dad. He was always affirming of her and would offer a different perspective than her mom did. Valerie's dad was instrumental in helping her accept herself. Valerie also found support from other queer students in her organizations. They allowed her space to talk about the issues she was facing and even though they did not have answers she was able to process and feel better about the situation. When things were extremely stressful, Valerie was able to cope by taking time to meditate and engage in physical exercise. Valerie overcame challenges facing her religious and sexual identity, and it took her much time and is on-going. Valerie attributed her reconciliation to her forcing herself to think about and process the conflicts, but also to giving herself time to figure it out.

CHAPTER 10: AUSTIN, THE (DIS)HONOR CODE OF CONDUCT

Austin (a pseudonym provided by the participant) was a senior anthropology major at a regional state university in the Midwest. He identified as gay and White-American, and was raised in an evangelical born-again Christian family that was very active in the church. Austin began his college career at a private Christian college in Indiana, but was asked to either withdraw from the institution or be expelled because his counselor reported his same-sex relationships. Austin dealt with much anger towards Christians and Christian organizations as he transferred to a new university where he found a group supportive of his sexual identity. Austin was an active leader within the LGBT student organization, and recently ended his first serious relationship. Austin longed for a relationship in his life, but realized it conflicted with him pursuing his life's goals. Austin shared his sexual identity with his family and it was an ongoing struggle for them to accept and support him and any same-sex relationship.

BACKGROUND

Traditional Christianity was not the norm for Austin; he grew up in a born-again evangelical church that moved in the "gifts of the Spirit." For those on the outside of this culture, it looked like people falling to the ground during prayer, people shaking and crying in church service, and hands raised high with unknown languages flowing loudly from people's mouths. Austin was at the front of his church youth group in this movement to embrace and be used by the Holy Spirit. At the age of five, Austin became a born-again Christian, and the church was his social space—where he gained his norms and found his friendship.

As early as the third grade, Austin recalled learning from parents and the church that homosexuality was wrong. Austin shared about his early thoughts on sexuality and gender:

I think the big thing that happened for me simultaneously was that I began to get picked on because I was effeminate because I didn't like sports....So, in my household it was you know taught to me starting in the third grade that homosexuality was a sin and that these people were not doing God's will and that all the sexual sins were disgusting...That was in third grade and in fourth grade they actually started using the words gay and fag and it made me really ashamed... Of course in seventh grade when hormones kicked I became more ashamed because I realized I actually was attracted to males.

Austin struggled as he became aware of his sexual orientation, and was afraid to share with anyone. Austin invested his time and efforts into extreme involvement with church; it was a way for him to escape the hate speech and the shame he had about his sexuality. He viewed his same-sex attraction as sin and we believed that God would redeem him from it.

Through Austin's emotional and spiritual struggles with his same-sex attraction he began to isolate himself. Austin shared:

I guess I felt like it was an inner battle all the time between my mind, my hormones, and what God's will was for me. I felt like I couldn't talk about it. So, I became very closed... I became very like compartmentalized and sexuality became this taboo topic in our household where you just didn't discuss it because that meant something wrong was going on.

Austin's same-sex attraction did not go away nor did his emotional distress. This struggle began to affect his social life and academics, so he began seeing a counselor for his depression As Austin moved into high school he was verbally harassed less, but his spiritual struggle lingered. During the ninth grade Austin was emotionally and spiritually sick, and began to reach out for help. Austin shared:

But then in high school I kept on having these attractions, these issues. I... purposefully stayed home from school one day because I was sick and in my mind it was like a spiritual sickness I felt all ashamed and this stuff and I was like I didn't want to go to school today. My parents let me stay home. I guess I took the whole time that day to pray and fast; I thought that I would write a letter to my parents saying, "I've had a lot of trouble with this issues with my sexuality, and I'm scared that I'm gonna be gay and go to hell." I put it on their bed and locked my door in my room and went to sleep. They were very scared that I had done something like very brutal...they didn't take the homosexuality very serious at first because in their mind they were like, "Oh this is a phase he is going through. Like if this sexuality thing doesn't work out we will just go to counseling."

Austin's parents turned to literature produced by James Dobson, which aimed to rid his same-sex attraction. The next few years of Austin's life focused on healing him from his sexual orientation.

Austin's parents did not disown him or reject him. Austin sometimes felt like they were excited that he was attracted to the same sex and viewed it as an opportunity for Jesus to show that he was powerful enough to heal their gay son. During this time of attempted healing, Austin's gender expression and sexual identity became a confusing problem for the family to resolve. Austin shared about his parents' philosophy:

...My dad and my mom...they would get down on themselves about it because James Dobson would often say, "Oh it's the parents fault. It was their doing. They did not raise the child up in a masculine enough way." I didn't know what to do with that. I was like, "I'm not trying to blame you I just want to change."

When the prayer alone did not resolve Austin's attraction they brought him to counseling at the church. The first pastor attributed his same-sex attractions to teenage hormones and pre-scribed prayer as the answer. Austin stated, "I was like, 'OK thanks; I don't know what to do with that. I've heard that several times already and whatever.'" By Austin's sophomore year of high school he gave up on the pastoral counseling and demanded his parents give him reparative therapy to get rid of his attractions towards the same-sex. Austin shared:

I told my parents, "This is not working. I am praying and all this stuff. I need intensive help. I need something reformatory..." So I started going to counselor who was a registered counselor... at our church... He had put me under a program what was called sexual addiction because he was an addiction counselor with relationships like when it comes to people having affairs and divorce issues. So I got labeled with a sexual addiction of homosexuality. That was the stance my family took on this issue.

Austin attended counseling for nearly two years to cure his same-sex attraction. The process exhausted him. His struggle with his sexuality greatly affected his religious and spiritual life. During his junior year he began to identify as an atheist, which later led to depression because the church was his coping mechanism. Later in high school, Austin recommitted his life to Jesus and began to identify as gay and Christian. He became very active in his high school Gay Straight Alliance, but was not romantically involved with any boys or men. Austin chose to attend a Christian college to pursue art. After starting college Austin began to be involved romantically with other men, but only during the summers. The challenges of being involved with men led to emotional, spiritual, and academic struggles.

RELATIONSHIPS: ACCEPTING YOUR LOSSES

Austin began to accept his sexual identity as a junior in high school, but did not get involved with other men until the summer after his first year of college. Austin's college, Evangel College (pseudonym) in Indiana, had an honor code which prohibited any same-sex romantic or physical involvement. Austin did not want to risk getting expelled, so he avoided dating men while in school. During the summer when he was home he reunited with a guy, Nolan (pseudonym), from his high school and church. Austin and Nolan were sexually involved at a party after they both drank vodka and smoked marijuana. Austin struggled to understand what to expect afterward. He shared:

And um, but then this being my first time I thought, "Oh we are going to be a couple now." And even though we had sex again at another party um there was very little communication between us and he pretty much told me I was just a party fuck. And that didn't feel too good.

Austin had no rules, norms, or ideas what to expect out of dating other men. He went into romantic involvement with unclear expectations, which often led to him being hurt. Due to Austin's school honor code, most of his romantic relationships involved random sexual activity with people at parties.

As Austin progressed in his college career, he began to embrace an activist mentality. Austin began to actively protest war, sexism, and mistreatment of the environment. He often felt alone in his classes when he advocated for marginalized populations, such as women or transgender people. During this time Austin was still identified as gay, but it was not a large part of his identity or his behaviors when he was at school. Austin's mentality changed and he began to get angry with Evangel College's practices; the college brought an ex-gay speaker to address the student body. The speaker shared his story of a drug addicted, gay, sex worker who was freed through Christianity. The speaker's story upset Austin because he felt like he portrayed all gay men negatively and narrowly. Austin felt like his sexuality was being attacked by his school and his friends in the audience supported the speaker. Austin shared how this incident affected his spiritual life:

I just feel like it pushed me over the edge back to rebelling against the Church. So for the next three semesters at Evangel College I was in the closet. I denied Christianity. I don't know what to do with that. I don't know why, but I think I still tried to have a relationship with God. I knew God was not the church and my spiritual ideas, but it really made me mad and at disgust with the church because it was God's people when they made these statements and divisions among themselves. I guess at times it made me very disillusioned with who the church was. At times I took a step further and said, "Well if the church is like this then who is this God who is supposed to be ruling over it? How is he even valid if his people are so screwed up?"

Austin struggled to separate his spiritual life from a religious organization that told him that he was sinful. This incident began to fuel the anger in Austin's life, but the following fall it escalated.

Austin thought studying abroad would give him some time to work through his frustrations with Evangel College, but he had to meet with a school counselor to approve his mental health before going abroad. This counseling session eventually led to Austin's expulsion. Austin shared this story:

But...these questions came up like, "Have you had sex? When was your first time? What was your first sexual encounter?" I was like, "Well, my first encounter was at a party with this guy from high school and there was alcohol and marijuana involved, yeah, that's my first experience..." That kind of got me into trouble. I thought that previously with counselors...that confidentiality was really taken to heart, but I guess because it was a private school and because they have a covenant of lifestyle commitment they had the ability to kind of hint to lean that I was someone they would look into further...I got called into the dean's office... They closed the door and they said asked me "Do you know why you are here?" "Something to do with study abroad?" They got kind of nervous. Then they asked me, "Do you know what happened on this date?" And it was the date of the night I slept with this guy. I was very appalled that that they had anything to do with that. I said, "Well, if you are asking then you probably already know." I became very defensive and I didn't know what to do. I got very angry I should have just cussed 'em out, but I tried to be very cool. And they said you have two options, "Either you withdraw and we tell everyone you have withdrawn from Evangel or we expel you and it is on your record."

Austin chose to withdraw, but dealt with extreme anger. He transferred to a public university near his parents' home. Austin was hindered academically, but he also suffered spiritually. Austin struggled to feel welcomed by anyone associated with Evangel College or Christianity. Austin discussed how his anger changed his perspective on religion:

There is still so much anger there...and the anger against, not the whole church, but people who have that mindset and think that homosexuality is a sin and think that they are right as Christians and to dictate to fellow Christians on how they should live their lives.. I thought I should really press into Jesus and Christianity like what to do with this (anger) and I think I learned a lot about grace through this and came back to Christ on my own terms on a personal spiritual level and not on a communal church thing. So, I guess I became more spiritual and less religious.

Through this tragic experience Austin began to refocus on his relationship with Jesus Christ. His pain from a Christian organization caused him to question his core religious beliefs.

In addition to Austin's conflicts with his religious college, he also struggled with his family's acceptance of his sexual orientation. Although he had been discussing his sexual identity with his parents for over five years, the discussions did not have the outcomes for which he hoped. Austin explained his parents' lack of support and acceptance:

They definitely pray that God's will for me is to remain celibate or to choose the route of self-proclaimed abstinence or God transforms me and that I marry a wife, um which causes a lot of tension at home. I try to be honest with them, but there are so many topics that if I were to discuss with them at home they would bring up a lot of guilt.

Austin valued the relationship he had with his parents and did not want to conceal parts of his life from them, but they continued to disagree about his sexual identity. Austin discovered a documentary which was a valuable resource to him as he was processing his religious identity and sexuality, and he wanted to share his new knowledge with his parents. When Austin saw the documentary which portrayed gay and lesbian people who identified as Christians, he gained hope. Austin arranged for his parents to watch the documentary, and he explained the situation further:

There is a movie called For the Bible Tells Me So, *and I watched it with my friend...So we watched the movie together and we were crying and hugging. I was like, "I think I can love Jesus more." She was like, "Yay." It was a very formative point for me because I thought that there was no really valid reasons why homosexuality could not fit into a proper Christian context...So I took it home and I got my parents and said, "I want you to watch this. It would mean a lot to me as your son because I am going through with this." The issue (his same-sex attraction) was not leaving, so I think they should get used to it and it will help them out. My dad left halfway through and I was like so mad at him. She (mom) watched to the end and was in tears at the end and we had like a three hour conversation at the end.*

The documentary discussed the Bible verses that addressed same-sex acts and provided interpretations that contradict the commonly believed interpretations, such as those that view same-sex relationships as unnatural, sinful abominations. Although Austin's mom watched the entire movie she still said she could not support his sexual identity or approve of his same-sex relationship. At the time, Austin's parents' opinions had great importance to him and his identity.

Austin struggled with feeling anger and sadness towards his parents, but later he felt apathetic towards their relationship. Austin's parents were uncomfortable with his criticism of his fundamentalist religious beliefs. When Austin began a serious relationship with another man last summer, he did not try to have him meet his parents because he knew they would refuse. Over the several years Austin dated men and identified as gay, his parents' lack of support and acceptance had changed little. His sexual identity caused strains in their relationship, and he hoped to one day have them support him. However, Austin seemed to care less and had less hope as time went on.

RESOLVING: A LITTLE AT A TIME

Austin had a number of conflicts to resolve, including his self-acceptance, his college community, and his family's approval. As a high school student Austin made significant growth in resolving his acceptance of his sexual orientation. After years of trying to remove any same-sex attraction, he began to accept them. Several teachers in high school inspired him, as they provided ideas about critical thinking and challenging ideologies that society holds to be normal. Austin's most significant moment of resolution came on Thanksgiving Day. He shared:

Over Thanksgiving I was watching this documentary of... people living and reenacting... the 1620s. There was this character on there who happened to be gay in the real world, but back then he couldn't show it because the law and he wanted to follow the historical laws back then which meant he couldn't speak of his homosexuality... I really associated myself with this guy, and I really took to it. I internalized what he was saying. As my parents called everyone in for prayer, I went to my room quickly. I just didn't feel like praying anymore. I closed the door, and I looked in front of the mirror... and said, "Austin, I'm gay." Instantly there was this weight that was lifted and I couldn't quit smiling... It was very pivotal. I constantly celebrate Thanksgivings now, so it's kind of like my coming out day or my self-acceptance day.

Austin struggled with different aspects of accepting his sexual orientation; however, most of his significant conflicts revolved around his family and religious organizations.

As Austin began to face separation from other students at Evangel College he sought out others who also felt like outcasts. Austin still interacted with those who disagreed with same-sex relationships, but he also found a group who would support him and understand his issues with the college and church. After Austin transferred to a public university, he quickly found a community to support his sexual identity. Austin became highly involved with the campus LGBT center. He had opportunities to feel included in a community and was able to openly share his internal and external challenges.

Austin did not feel like his family ever became supportive of his sexual orientation even while repeatedly challenging them.

Austin was pleased that they stopped trying to change him. As Austin faced challenges with gaining his family's approval and support he relied on other systems of support. Austin described finding support and community from other sources such as his friends from work, his LGBT student organization, and his friends in the artist community. There were a variety of other resources Austin found helpful as he resolved his challenges with his religious and sexual identities. Even though Austin has had negative experiences with counselors, he still stated that counseling was a tremendous support for him; counseling taught him how to process conflict. Austin recommended that campuses should regularly talk about religion because he found few spaces where he could express his religious identity and his sexual identity comfortably.

Austin was able to share how he resolved immense struggle with self-acceptance, family acceptance, and condemnation from his religious college. Austin turned these challenges into an opportunity to make a difference. Austin regularly shared his story around campus and the community about being expelled for being gay. Austin served as a peer mentor at the university LGBT center; he provided basic resources to students questioning their sexual orientation. Austin also became an executive board member in the LGBT student organization. Austin quickly settled into his new college community where he was able to educate the campus community about inclusion of LGBT people. During Austin's second year at his new university he studied abroad in Morocco, and planned to take his LGBT activism to the Middle East after he graduated.

CHAPTER 11: REBECCA, BURNING UP CONFESSION

Rebecca (a pseudonym provided by the participant) was a freshman at a private liberal arts college in a Los Angeles suburb and identified as bisexual. She was multiracial, Latina and White-American, and her dad's Mexican ethnicity kept her from sharing her sexual identity with him. Rebecca grew up heavily involved in a Catholic Church near San Francisco and her religion was a significant part of her life. Rebecca began dating women during the middle of high school and recently ended a relationship with a woman four years older than she. Rebecca just finished her first semester of college and was still trying to adjust to her busy college life. Rebecca struggled with her bisexual identity because of negative messages she received from her family, and she struggled to feel like her life was pleasing to God. Rebecca spent a period of time hating herself and wanting to change. As she tried to reconcile her identities she turned to the church for affirmation, but was emotionally and spiritually torn apart. Rebecca was also publicly condemned with her girlfriend, which left her distraught and with no one to support her.

BACKGROUND: SEEKING PERFECTION

Rebecca was highly involved with her church for as long as she could remember. She was an active part of the weekly services, she represented the church in public spaces, and she was one of the founders of the youth group. Most people saw her as the perfect daughter within her congregation and it was not rare that congregation members would tell her parents how perfect she was. Rebecca shared:

They only saw the miss goody two-shoes, 3.8 GPA or above, awesome. Like everyone would say to my dad, "I wish my daughter was just like yours. You are so lucky to have Rebecca as your daughter. Can I adopt your daughter?" Apparently I was the perfect daughter at church.

Rebecca was proud of her reputation at church, but feared they would find out her secret of being bisexual. Rebecca came out in high school as bisexual and began her first romantic relationship with one of her best friends. When she was sexually involved with another girl for the first time it felt natural, but she also had what she calls a "freak out" moment. Rebecca explained further:

We would look at each other and think, "Oh shit. I have feelings for her. What am I gonna do with these feelings?"... We look at each other and I start panicking. I walk by her and I go to my locker and sitting at my locker and I am having a panic attack... I am literally sitting on the floor in the fetal position in the hallway. I was freaking out and she looks at me and I just get up and run away... I was trying to calm myself down first off. Why was I freaking out? I couldn't figure it out. It is just a girl. This was the first girl I ever had feelings for. I was like, "Oh my God! Is it supposed to be this way?" I don't think I was supposed to feel this way.

Rebecca was able to overcome her panic attack and move forward with the girl she was interested in dating and they began a relationship. Although she managed to resolve the immediate situation, the insecurities and confusion of her sexual identity did not resolve quickly.

Rebecca decided to tell her mom about her attraction to women and her newly accepted bisexual identity. Rebecca's mom was supportive of her being attracted to women, but did not validate her bisexuality. Rebecca shared more about her conversation with her mom:

Then I told her and she said "OK that is fine," but she doesn't believe in bisexuality. That kinda, I don't want to say upset me, but it confused me. I was like how do you not believe it? I am bisexual. She went on to say that, "You will choose one or the other. You will be a lesbian or you will be straight. There is no in between."

Rebecca's older brother agreed with her mom and would often criticize her identity. Other people in her life just assumed she was experimenting, which made her upset because they never would view her relationships as real or serious. Other people's crit-icisms of her sexual identity made her sometimes doubt if her bisexuality was real. Rebecca spent years trying to under-stand her sexual identity while also trying to prove her authen-ticity to others.

RELATIONSHIPS: SOCIETY AND THE CHURCH REINFORCING INTERNAL HOMOPHOBIA

As Rebecca began dating her first girlfriend, Elsbeth (pseudo-nym), it felt natural and she wanted to continue to pursue it; however, she had many moments of confusion and doubt. Religion was a central part of Rebecca's life, and she wanted to ensure she was pleasing God with her life. Sometimes during church she would sit and listen to the message and feel extreme guilt because she felt like she was living a lie to her church and her God. One message at church resonated with her for some time. She explained further:

It was about being true to your body and your body is a temple if you don't know what is inside of it then you don't know yourself and God won't know who you are… I felt like the homily or the gospel was aimed at me especially when Elsbeth would be there.

Although Rebecca's church viewed her as the perfect Catholic teenager, she viewed herself very differently. Rebecca struggled with extreme internal distress because of her sexuality. Rebecca explained:

The whole body is the temple, was like yeah I've messed with my body more than the church should know, so I still struggled with the depression thing. I used to cut ... I have scarred my body and done so much to my body and like I have had sex with girls... I can't change what I have already done, and I felt really guilty about that.

Rebecca struggled to be at peace with herself and with God. She wondered why she had these attractions, if God made her this way, was God angry with her, and why would he do that to her? Rebecca wanted to be what she thought was normal, so she wanted to be heterosexual. Her anguish and doubt turned to her physically harming herself on a regular basis. Rebecca's longtime struggle with depression intensified, consuming her thoughts and emotions.

As Rebecca tried to accept her sexual identity, she was seeking affirmation from her church; she went to the priest to discuss her relationship with Elsbeth. However, Rebecca's doubt escalated after speaking with the priest. Rebecca shared:

Since I am so rooted in Catholicism, in my religion, I wanted the church to be OK with me. I wanted it really badly. I wanted it to be OK. I wanted to be told that "It was going to be OK and that you would be accepted no matter what," but obviously it didn't happen. It really broke me and my religion for the longest time... I told him because I wanted reassurance. I wanted to know the religion I was in would accept me for me.

Rebecca did not receive reassurance from her church community Rebecca received negative reactions from the priest which greatly affected her identity, self-acceptance, and relationship. She shared more:

I was like, "Is it OK that I have thoughts of people of the same sex," and he basically told me no I was going to hell. The Bible thought I was wrong... That priest had a huge effect on me. That guy messed with my head so much. Like (he) told me I was going to hell and that it was disgusting... It was still really hard for me to accept... I was actually holding back tears and when I turned around and left the priest I just broke down. I was broken for a while because that is who I was. I think about people of the same sex and my own religion doesn't accept that. Who am I anymore? I was really really torn apart.

After the conversation with the priest, Rebecca began to question her identity and relationship with Elsbeth. She was conflicted because she wanted her religion, religious community, and her relationship with Elsbeth. She explained more of her reaction:

That was a big reason why I would question so much and why I didn't want to be gay because society was and is mostly straight, so I was like what am I supposed to do? I can't change who I am so I would hate myself.... I was upset and I didn't want anything to do with the Church for a while...

Rebecca still attended church after the incident, but she struggled to feel included and accepted by the one community she most valued.

Rebecca and her girlfriend faced another incident of condemnation while in public, but it was by a stranger who disapproved of two women being affectionate in public. They were at a Christmas tree lighting in a park in San Francisco, and a lady told them their relationship was inappropriate and against God and the Bible. The incident was very difficult for Rebecca to get over, but it did not seem to affect her girlfriend. Rebecca shared about the incident, "I just couldn't get over it... I was pissed. I was hurt. What is this woman why is this woman telling me I can't be cuddling with my girlfriend. I was way confused."

As Rebecca faced condemnation from the priest and from the stranger she had a range of emotions. She reacted with sadness, hurt, anger, and doubt. Rebecca wanted her girlfriend to support her, but Elsbéth did not understand how much it affected her and just laughed it off. As Rebecca faced challenges reconciling her religious and sexual identities, she often found that her girlfriend did not understand and was unable to support her.

RESOLVING: SEEKING OUT SUPPORT AND BEING SELF-RELIANT

Rebecca faced intense challenges as she tried to find support for her same-sex relationship and often struggled to find a place that could support her. Rebecca felt that she could not always rely on her family or even her girlfriend, but she did find support from her close friends. After the incident with the priest, Rebecca told several of her friends. They were supportive of her and tried to understand her pain. Rebecca's friends were able to affirm her identity and confirm the priest was wrong. She needed these people, so she could express her hurt and also to reinforce God's love for her. Rebecca felt supported on her campus; she disclosed her relationship slowly, but always received positive reactions from those around her. Through numerous positive reactions to her sexual identity she began to feel a part of a community and normal.

Although Rebecca did not receive affirmation from her church, she did receive affirmation from the lesbian, gay, bisexual, and transgender student organization on campus. She was able to lead discussions and build leadership skills while also having a supportive outlet to work through identity issues. The student organization also provided Rebecca with a mentor who had resolved some similar issues and was able to provide support to her as she faced challenges.

Despite finding numerous sources of support, Rebecca often felt like there was no one to help her resolve her issues, so she became self-reliant. Rebecca explained:

I got myself through most of the stuff. I had one or two friends who were very supportive of me, but other than that everyone was kinda ignoring it like it is just a relationship and I will do what I want to do... I don't like taking help from people, so usually it is hard for me to be in a relationship in that sense because they want to help me get through that, but I am usually a person who needs to get over it myself... I was the support of her and I was the support of myself.

Many people assumed her bisexuality was just a phase and—as she struggled with both her religion and relationship—people did not take it seriously. One of the ways in which Rebecca supported herself was through writing. She explained further:

I write a lot... that is how I get my thoughts out clearly when I try to get out my emotions, thoughts, or feelings... if I want something to come across the way I want, then I write it. I also write a lot of poetry and when I am not in the mood for poetry and really angry I just vent the stream of consciousness and write and write and write. It doesn't make sense, but it helps and I can go back and read it and figure out what happened and it makes me feel a whole lot better and I can relax and breathe.

Rebecca dealt with depression, self-hatred, and fear of rejection as she tried to find peace within her religious and sexual identities. She was still in the process of resolving her challenges as a freshman; however, she was finding ways of resolving her challenges. Rebecca was building a support system and finding ways in which to manage her internal struggles.

Chapter 12: Conclusion, Inclusive and Active Support

Educational, religious, and social service organizations cannot ignore their own claims to be inclusively support all people; individuals embody complex and intersecting identity categories. In order to effectively serve all students, organizational and institutional practices, procedures, and climates must be examined fully, revised, and updated to reflect the ever-present diverse populations. The stories in this book described the many issues people might face in communities, and also clearly stated what resources they needed in order to survive and succeed during their educational experiences. These students' conflicts revolved around issues with family, trying to hide their same-sex relationships, seeking community support, trying to overcome negative socialization, and doubting the morality of their same-sex relationships.

Seeking Family Support

Having their same-sex relationships accepted by their family members was a major concern for the students in this book. These students faced struggles as extreme as attempts to cast out demons and as subtle as microaggressive attacks that invalidated the significance of a partner. The experiences of these students affected their emotional life and their academic life in some instances. Tyler became depressed as he battled his mother's disapproval and was placed on academic probation. Austin became emotionally overwhelmed and avoided going to class. The participants were attempting to resolve complex identity issues and having the approval of their family would have made their developmental challenges easier; however, some of them were not supported or were attacked by family members, which escalated their identity development issues.

As many parents felt uncomfortable with their student's sexual identity and/or same-sex relationship, they avoided discussing the issue, person, or relationship. The students often wanted to freely discuss their life with their family, but were not given that option because of their family's discomfort with same-sex relationships. The heterosexism and homophobia these participants faced was subtle, but repetitive and detrimental to the building of positive self-identity. It is the role of the higher education institution to ensure the student is fully supported in order to succeed interpersonally and academically. If the student needs support from family members in order to succeed, the institution should provide family members with the knowledge and skills necessary to support their student.

As parents and family members prepare to send their student to college they should be provided with knowledge about sexual diversity. Many institutions have parent orientations, and discussions about student identity development should be integrated in orientation sessions. Multicultural centers, diversity offices, and LGBT centers should ensure their publications and web sites include resources for parents and family members. As students return home for breaks, parents and families may observe changes, and be unsure how to understand or respond to the students' identity development process. Parents and family members should be provided with basic information around terminology, common emotional struggles, and campus resources. Parents and family members should be introduced to their local or regional PFLAG (Parents, Families, and Friends of Lesbians and Gays) chapter. Parents and families may also be struggling to make sense of their student's identity and discussing the family's concerns with others who are having similar experiences can be beneficial.

Post-secondary educators should be cognizant of complex family dynamics and the support or lack of support students may experience from their families. It is important to provide opportunities for students to discuss their interpersonal challenges as students undergo a variety of emotional dilemmas. As students are planning to return home for holidays or breaks, they may have more anxiety around spending time with their families, as well as being away from their LGBT community. Participants, such as Mark and Jenna, felt as if their LGBT campus community was their primary support system, so knowing that support will not be present for several months may cause anxiety

Supporting young non-heterosexual adults as they face difficult life changes is the responsibility of higher education, community agencies, and families. They should work collaboratively to ensure families are aware and prepared to support their children. Although the lack of information may seem subtle—micro-aggressive attacks seem minute—the impact is drastic and many of the students in this situation consider and/or attempt suicide. Family members must recognize the seriousness of developing a positive non-heterosexual identity and the challenges which come with it. Family members cannot expect it to be only educational institution's responsibility, but through the partnership between educational organizations and families, Christian college-students in same-sex relationships can face these challenges with support and guidance from multiple sources.

Many non-heterosexual people turn elsewhere to receive support they originally wanted from their family. Some family members are resentful because their young adult does not share aspects of hir, her, or his life with the family; however, the young non-heterosexual adult may be in need of support, and will find it somewhere in order to survive overwhelming emotional stress. Family members must commit to ongoing education, unlearning, and patience as the non-heterosexual student tries to find support

HIDING RELATIONSHIPS

A number of the participants chose to hide their relationships; they hid them from parents, siblings, churches, and their educational institutions. Some of them chose to hide them for physical safety, some chose to hide them to avoid emotional distress and isolation, and some chose to hide their same-sex relationship in order to remain at their Christian university. Valerie hid her relationship in order to salvage some type of relationship with her mother, and after unsuccessfully hiding her relationship from her girlfriend's mother the relationship ended. As the students transitioned to campus they were unsure of the climate for non-heterosexual people, so they evaluated the acceptance of same-sex relationships before exposing themselves and their relationships.

As the students hid significant parts of their life they became stressed. The students had to avoid being physically affectionate in public spaces in order to avoid being harassed, condemned, or facing social isolation. The pressure of hiding a relationship strained both partners and was often too much to handle. Engaging in serious interpersonal relationships is a key part of college student development (Chickering & Reisser, 1993), and a student should not feel forced to hide a key part of her or his college life. The stigma of being in a same-sex relationship on a college campus has real consequences. In a recent study by Rankin, Weber, Blumenfeld, and Frazer (2010), they found that 21% of non-heterosexual identified students faced harassment on their campus because of their sexual orientation.

Schools should understand that many members of the LGBTQ community may hide their sexual identity and/or same-sex relationship. Forty-three percent of college students stated that they chose to hide their sexual identity and/or gender identity to avoid intimidation (Rankin, Weber, Blumenfeld, & Frazer, 2010) In order to protect students from hate and bias incidents, institutions should continue to educate their campus about the prevalence of hate and bias related incidents. Institutions should create and promote systems to report hate and bias incidents. Organizational administrators, faculty members, and students need to be educated on what constitutes a hate crime, hate incident, and bias incident as well as how to report it and how to intervene.

As students hid their relationships on campus they often felt unsure of where to go in order to feel safe enough to be open about their same-sex relationships. Many campuses have student organizations and support groups; however, some students may not know how to find them. LGBTQ student organizations are crucial for students to network, support one another, and create social and leadership opportunities (Windmeyer, 2006). Campuses should ensure LGBTQ student organizations exist on their campuses and support them as they recruit and support new students. These student organizations provide political action, social support, and educational initiatives (Scott, 1991). As student organizations, they may need advising from faculty or staff members to create the organizations and develop effective leadership models and programs.

Christian campuses with strict honor codes prohibiting same-sex relationships cause all students in same-sex relationships to hide or face expulsion. LGBTQ allies at these institutions should adamantly challenge policies and advocate for students facing marginality and discrimination. Allies are important to the support systems that LGBTQ college students utilize as they navigate their campuses (Windmeyer, 2006). Supporting students as they are choosing to hide or quit hiding is necessary because the consequences greatly affect their academic career. Educators should encourage students to organize and challenge institutional policies. Educators should empower the students to make decisions on their own and help them evaluate and understand the consequences of their decisions. Students and educators at religious institutions should become well-informed of the various interpretations of biblical scriptures addressing same-sex relationships, and use the new knowledge to challenge policies.

It is important to understand students' decisions to expose their same-sex relationships or sexual identity on their own terms as educators work with a variety of students. If a student openly identifies as non-heterosexual in one setting or leads an LGBTQ group it does not mean ze, she, or he openly identifies as such in all spaces. Educators should challenge sexual identity development models, such as Cass' (1979), and aim to comprehend the complexity of "coming-out." The "coming-out" process happens over a lifetime and on a daily basis. Students take risks each time they choose to expose their sexual identity and same-sex relationship, so the decision to identify should be left to them and their decisions should be supported.

Students often choose to hide their relationships because they receive messages that it is unsafe and unacceptable to reveal them. Serious measures must be taken in order for an institution to prove that it is a climate where students can be open about their relationships. Institutions need to have visible and positive faculty and staff members, so students can see well-adjusted adults who represent a variety of identities including those who also feel safe to be open about their religious identities. Higher education institutions need to have upper administrators who are comfortable with LGBTQ communities and make the time to support their initiatives and events. Policies and procedures that protect and include non-heterosexual people is the minimum a university should be providing; the campus community should actively celebrate the lives, accomplishments, research, and teachings of LGBTQ people.

SEEKING COMMUNITY SUPPORT

As students made sense of their sexual and religious identities, they often felt isolated from their communities. Within Christian communities they faced discrimination, hate, and rejection. Some students experienced public condemnation by religious community members and some felt pain as religious leaders disapproved of their same-sex relationships. Many of the students left their religious communities permanently or temporarily as they attempted to resolve the conflicts of their religion and sexuality. Some participants sought new religious communities that were more supportive of their multiple identities. Participants also shared being isolated and condemned within their LGBTQ communities. Their religion was often mocked and used as an identity that categorized them as oppressors and resistant to queer and gay rights. As Valerie and He Joonie, for example, faced ridicule due to their religious beliefs, they felt isolated and rejected within the LGBTQ community.

The students in this book felt isolated within both of their communities and never fully accepted or understood. Astin (1984) discussed that if students do not have connections to their institution they are less likely to persist until graduation, and Astin's findings have been the foundation of student affairs education for decades. However, few attempts have been made to get diverse non-heterosexual students connected to their institutions. Additionally, 33% of non-heterosexual college students reported that they considered leaving their college due to a challenging climate (Rankin, Weber, Blumenfeld, & Frazer, 2010). All students should feel welcomed and included on their campuses, but many Christian students who are LGBTQ identified feel isolated within all communities of which they are members.

Campuses should offer spaces for Christian and other religious LGBTQ students. A sense of community and acceptance is important as students undergo complex transitions, and creating spaces for students to feel fully accepted is crucial to their positive well-being. Students involved with religious organizations may have questions and want to know that others are in similar situations. A support group or a shared space to support one another can create a new sense of community and combat feelings of isolation. Support groups can also occur through websites; some Christian students needing support may fear exposing their sexual identity or relationship due to the negative stigma in the religious community. Discussion about religion and sexuality should be promoted and facilitated on a regular basis in order to create open and safe spaces on campus. Discussing religion is often avoided in order to not offend people, but it should be openly discussed in a tone where people can learn from each other. Both religion and sexuality are often considered taboo topics, but open discussion of religion and sexuality should be embraced as they provide critical pieces to the complex identities of college students.

Religious organizations and campus ministries should regularly be encouraged to participate in diversity and social justice events and programs. Many campuses offer LGBTQ education workshops, safe zone or safe space initiatives, and religious organizations should be invited. Campus life and religious life offices should be aware of religious organizations that are openly affirming of same-sex relationships and should promote the information to students.

As LGBTQ student organizations aim to create inclusive climates, policies, and procedures on campus, they should be provided knowledge on oppression, anti-oppressive activism, and social justice. If the student organizers had adequate understanding of the multiple forms of oppression and how they are connected they may be less oppressive to their religious peers.

LGBTQ student organizations often believe the stereotypes about Christians and mistreat the entire group based of generalizations. LGBTQ student organizations must challenge their own understandings and also be inclusive of those who have strong religious identities. As student organizers, they should be aware of the multiple identities each person has and how these identities can be more or less salient. LGBTQ organizations and spaces should provide opportunities for students to discuss other aspects of their identity including their religious, spiritual, racial, ethnic, class, and gender identities.

The goals of religious organizations and LGBTQ organizations are to support their members and encourage them to grow in their respective identities; however, they need to be aware of the full identities of their members and seek to create organizations that are truly accepting of people. The limited understanding these groups have of Christians in same-sex relationships will lead their members to reject their organizations and isolate them from those who are supposed to be there for support. Each of these groups' exclusiveness causes individuals to dichotomize their sexual and religious identities, which leads to further anxiety and emotional distress.

DECONSTRUCTING SOCIALIZATION

The students in this book continued to battle negative ideas about their sexual identity and images of same-sex relationships. They continued to question if they were born with same-sex attractions or if they had somehow been damaged through poor parenting. The negative socialization about their identities and relationships were one of the most challenging aspects to overcome, and it affected many aspects of their lives. The emotional challenges led to depression, self-hatred, and suicidal ideations. As non-heterosexual students are making sense of their sexual identity they may experience guilt, self-hatred, and depression (Buchanan, Dzelme, Harris, & Hecker, 2001); moreover, when they are also faced with a lifetime of religious socialization telling them they were abominations, the negative emotions can intensify. Even as the students were able to embrace their sexual identity, some of them felt that they must abandon their religious identity when they identified with a non-heterosexual identity.

According to D'Augelli's life span model (1994), as lesbian, gay and bisexual youth are claiming their sexual identity they must challenge any pre-conceived ideas they have about lesbian, gay, or bisexual people. Most of the participants did not perceive LGBTQ people to have religious identities or be Christians. Through religion, media, and other aspects of society, they had only seen a one-dimensional, limited representation of LGBTQ people. Several of the male participants stated that they perceived being gay synonymously with being very sexually active. The participants felt pressured to have sex randomly, which often put their health at risk. Institutions should continue to educate students about safer sex practices as well as promote and provide regular testing for sexually transmitted infections.

As campuses become aware of the intense emotional turmoil that Christian students in same-sex attractions encounter, they must create opportunities for students to receive the support necessary to their personal and academic well-being. The students battling negative images about their identity had difficult times engaging in classes and campus communities. More than one-third of them planned or attempted suicides because they believed they could not be loved by God. The intense struggles the students faced should be addressed as campuses aim to holistically heal and support student development. Educators as well as student leaders should be trained to identify signs of suicide and ways in which to prevent suicides. Open discussions about suicide should happen within LGBTQ communities in an effort for community members to support one another. Several of the students who discussed their suicidal ideations said they had the most serious thoughts or attempts near the beginning of the academic year.

Faculty and staff should be aware of the additional stresses of transitioning to college and the loneliness and isolation that can be intensified during this time. LGBTQ community events should be scheduled frequently during the early period of each academic year.

The Bible was used as the primary method for delivering negative ideas about same-sex relationships. As the students learned new ways in which to read the Bible and new interpretations of scriptures discussing same-sex relationships, they began to construct a more positive image of themselves and their relationships. Bible analysis and study groups with focus on LGBTQ people and issues can greatly help open dialogue and create opportunities for critical Bible reading. Partnerships with local openly affirming churches can rebuild positive images of churches, so students feel safe embracing their religious identities.

Media is a significant factor in socializing students, and participants brought up many aspects of media that were helpful and hurtful to their identity development. Two documentaries that students often discussed as being extremely beneficial to them as they reconciled their religious and sexual identities were *Fish Out of Water* and *For the Bible Tells Me So*. Campuses should use these documentaries for open screenings and discussions as well as make them available in libraries for individual student use. Additionally, as campuses show films on campus residence hall channels or through student activities, they should ensure they are showing movies that portray diverse couples—including those who are in same-sex relationships. The media's subtle heteronormativity reinforces the socialization LGBTQ youth have received since birth.

Most of the students did not know that they could have their Christian identity coexist with a same-sex relationship; they had not seen this in the lives of people around them or in the media.

LGBTQ students on college campuses have stated their desire to have faculty and staff role models within their communities to provide support (Windmeyer, 2006). These role models need to embrace multiple identities and feel comfortable sharing more aspects of their complex identities than only their sexual identity. As students met older Christian people in same-sex relationships they found hope that they too could balance their religious and sexual identity. Institutions should ensure they are hiring diverse faculty and staff members who can serve as role models to students from marginalized backgrounds. Campuses need to create opportunities for students, faculty, and staff to connect outside of the classroom. Programs for older students, faculty members, and staff members to mentor younger students should be created in order to build community, improve visibility, and provide individual support. Kraig (1998) found that LGBT faculty and staff mentors were vital assets to students as they shared their life stories and assisted in navigating university resources and structures. Additionally, programming that includes students, faculty, and staff on panels or telling stories about their identities, struggles, and support systems should be created in order for students undergoing struggles with their identity to see and hear adequate representation from people with similar experiences. The panels should intentionally plan for the panelists to represent a variety of identities including those from multiple marginalized groups.

The students in this book faced a variety of emotional struggles and often turned to counseling in order to resolve and make sense of their religious identities and same-sex relationships. Some of the students were concerned about their counselor's ability to support students through challenges with their sexual identity, religious identity, or both. Counselors on college campuses should receive specialized training in order to become familiar with issues that non-heterosexual students often face as well as how those issues might intersect with other aspects of their identity. Counselors should ensure students know they are open, welcoming, and prepared to handle complex issues such as those that affect a student's religious or sexual identities. Counseling services was one of the most frequently stated assets to the participants as they encountered challenges engaging in same-sex relationships, but many were initially hesitant to visit counselors. Educators must be aware of their counseling services ability to cater to diverse populations, and challenge centers to further expand the services they provide. If the campus counseling services cannot meet the needs of LGBTQ students, then local community resources should be identified and shared with the students.

DOUBTING THE MORALITY OF THE RELATIONSHIP

It is a significant part of human development to engage in serious romantic relationships, but some of the participants were unable to focus on the joyful part of their human development due to doubts that they were displeasing God with their same-sex relationship. These doubts were common for most of the participants during early parts of the relationships, but some of them continued to struggle with these fears throughout. The participants doubted if two people of the same sex should be romantically involved and/or sexually involved. Guilt, shame, and doubt caused their relationships to struggle.

As students face relationship challenges, those challenges can create turmoil in other aspects of their lives. Current society is heteronormative and higher education exists within the same framework. Campuses need to ensure that they support the unions and partnerships of same-sex couples by showing institutional support. Institutional policies for students, faculty, and staff should include benefits for partnerships of all combinations, and it should be made known to the community that the institution values same-sex relationships. Non-discrimination policies should include both sexual orientation and gender identity; policy inclusion promotes an LGBTQ-friendly culture, which greatly affects the climate for students, faculty, and staff (Windmeyer, 2006). These feelings of doubt are filtered from national climates as well. Marriage laws and immigration laws reinforce the stigma associated with same-sex relationships as they invalidate the normality, legitimacy, and significance of same-sex relationships.

Many of the doubts the students receive are from on-going exposure to only opposite-sex relationships through television, magazines, and books. As campuses plan social events they should include films that feature a variety of types of romantic relationships and reinforce the positive aspects of two people of the same sex being in healthy relationships. Classrooms should ensure curriculum is inclusive of multiple types of relationships. To ensure student activities planners and classroom instructors are aware of the negative reinforcement of same-sex relationships, they should be provided with educational work-shops on a regular schedule. Assisting students to overcome doubts and heteronormative thinking takes much effort and time. The ongoing socialization that same-sex relationships are in-ferior occurs throughout many venues on a college campus.

FURTHER CONSIDERATIONS FOR EDUCATIONAL, COMMUNITY, AND RELIGIOUS ORGANIZATIONS

The challenges students faced stemmed from many aspects of their identities, which included their religious, sexual, racial, and gender identities. As students encountered emotional issues, physical harassment, isolation, and condemnation, they faced stress and anxiety, which affected not only their personal life, but also their relationships and academics. As the students aimed to resolve their conflicts, they found a variety of resources and activities which aided them.

Several of the students wanted and needed someone with whom to share their struggles. Many of the students turned to close friends or siblings; as they expressed their challenges, making sense of their religious life and same-sex relationship, they felt relieved. A number of the students found student affairs administrators who worked full-time in campus LGBT centers as useful assets. Many students looking for university resources quickly find an LGBT center as a visible place of support and a way in which to connect with others (Windmeyer, 2006). They gained insights through a professionally educated administrator who understood LGBT college student development and how it intersects with other identities. Colleges and universities should ensure they have full-time staffed LGBTQ centers or a minimum of an administrator focused on gender and sexuality within a diversity or multicultural office. When students knew of no other place to turn and were distraught, they often turned to the campus LGBT administrator.

As the students faced extreme distress they often turned to methods which would help them process their feelings and release emotion. Some participants discussed physical exercise, meditation, and art as effective ways to relieve the stresses of managing their conflicts with their religious identity and their same-sex relationship. Institutions should provide regular stress relief programs and LGBT organizations and offices should partner with health and wellness initiatives in order to create spaces that LGBT identified students feel welcomed. Providing opportunities for students to paint, write, and engage in musical activities can let students express their emotions in ways that are not harmful to themselves. Supporting Christian students in same-sex relationships as well as other students who are emotionally distressed due to challenges that occur during their academic experiences is not limited to only one office or organization on campus. Effective collaboration from multiple offices, organizations, and departments is necessary in order to ensure students are holistically supported and can fully engage in their higher education institutions.

COMMUNITY COLLEGES

Community colleges must also consider the implications for Christian students in same-sex relationships. Most community colleges do not have LGBTQ centers or active LGBTQ student organizations; therefore, students facing struggles may have no resources. Community colleges must ensure students are well supported even if there are fewer student life opportunities. As many students are not living in the residence halls there are fewer opportunities for outreach, education, and advocacy for those being oppressed. Community colleges should work collaboratively with local LGBT organizations as well as openly affirming churches if available in order to provide resources. As transfer counselors are working with students they should be aware of four-year universities that offer supportive environments for LGBTQ students. However, one of the key assets the Christian college students stated as beneficial was having a post-secondary educator share words of support and encouragement. Community colleges should ensure they have faculty and staff members who are willing to serve as positive representations and mentors for students. Community colleges should also provide on-going training about gender and sexual diversity for faculty and staff members, so the campus community can identify students who are struggling with identity issues.

SECONDARY EDUCATION

Many of the participants described having severe emotional distress in middle school and high school. During these times they faced bullying based on gender expression and perceived sexual orientation. As the participants also realized they were having same-sex attractions they went into extreme depression, isolation, and self-hatred. Secondary education faculty, staff, and counselors must be prepared to address issues which could lead to withdrawal, self-harm, or even suicide attempts. Secondary educators and parents or guardians must be able to educate one another as they aim to support non-heterosexual and non-gender conforming youth. Counselors must be educated on how to serve students who are not heterosexual, who are not gender conforming, and who also have strong spiritual and religious identities. Some of the participants were already sexually active in high school, but with little or no education about safer and healthier practices. Secondary educators must provide adequate safer sex knowledge, which is inclusive of all types of relationships.

RELIGIOUS ORGANIZATIONS

Religious organizations will continue to isolate congregation members if they approach same-sex couples with hate and bias. Many religious organizations also view non-gender conforming people as sinners and assume they are gay or lesbian identified. Churches, Bible studies, and student ministries must reexamine and critically analyze their understandings of same-sex relationships by seeking out diverse interpretations of the key scriptures discussing texts on same-sex relationships.

A variety of religious organizations currently operate on a "Don't ask: Don't tell" mentality; however, many people will still feel marginalized by those organizations because of the heteronormativity and current negative reputation of Christian organizations. Christian organizations need to further examine their views on social justice through a Christ-like lens while placing a focus on historically marginalized groups such as people of color, women, the poor, and non-heterosexual people.

Churches that make statements about being openly affirming of same-sex relationships need to do more than simply make a statement and provide a rainbow decal on their signage. Church leaders must be examples and also provide educational opportunities for congregation members to further understand LGBTQ identity and societal issues that come along with LGBTQ identity. Churches must examine their traditions and not only ensure that they are not homophobic but that they are also not heterosexist. LGBTQ identities and issues include more than just marriage and military services; thus, social justice organizations that support LGBTQ members should be aware of the vast forms of racism, sexism, classism, ableism, and homophobia that affects LGBTQ people. Churches should be free of hate crimes, hate incidents, bias-related incidents, as well as microaggressive attacks.

SOCIAL SERVICES ORGANIZATIONS

Social services organizations that serve those receiving counseling services, crises response, and community resources need to understand the complexity of identity and relationships. As they are providing social services they must first realize that not all people are in heterosexual relationships and also that some of these non-heterosexual people may have strong religious identities that influence all aspects of their lives. The counseling services that these people may be seeking could be related to conflicts with their multiple identities, such as those between their religious and sexual identities. Social service providers must be aware of the common struggles that Christians in same-sex relationships experience.

SOCIAL JUSTICE COMMUNITY ORGANIZATIONS

Campus and community social justice organizations can often place a large focus on race, but ignore other salient pieces of oppressed groups' identities, such as sexual identity and religious identity. Social justice organizations must continuously challenge their understanding of identity intersections and best practices on ways in which to engage diverse populations. Social justice community organizations have large influences as they train law enforcement officers, educators, and community leaders; therefore, they should be aware of the conflicts associated with religion and sexuality.

LGBTQ COMMUNITY ORGANIZATIONS

Many cities or communities have LGBTQ community organizations, but the organizations can often have limited understanding of the diversity of the LGBTQ community, which often excludes people of color and religious people. LGBTQ community organizations must actively seek to improve its services and image as it relates to communities of color and religious organizations. LGBTQ community organizations should actively collaborate with community organizations which serve people of color and religious groups to demonstrate their understanding of complex identities. Many Christian non-heterosexual people feel threatened within LGBT spaces, so conversations about religion should be encouraged and celebrated.

CLOSING THOUGHTS

The stories shared about making sense of Christianity and loving someone of the same-sex were tragic, heartbreaking, and inspiring. There are many stories not included in this book and those narratives go untold and ignored. The students who shared their stories of pain and triumph displayed bravery and a commitment to creating a new environment other youth. After I shared some of these stories at a speaking engagement the word began to spread. I regularly received calls, e-mails, and Face-book messages from people in desperate places hating them-selves and wanting to end their lives. Things might be getting better, but only for some and at a dreadfully slow pace. In order for substantial change to occur people from all religious, sexual, gender, race, and political backgrounds must put their love and concern into action. Limiting our actions to positive thinking and progressive ideologies fall short of creating communities where all people feel welcomed, loved, and supported.

These stories may seem rare or even extreme, but so many more remain hidden. Sexuality is taboo to discuss in most social settings and religion is even more rarely discussed in today's climate. There are few places for people confused about their religion, sexuality, and spirituality to process conflicts and find support. These students' stories are the few that turned their pain into action. These students turned oppression into activism and are leading their generation towards a new society; one that celebrates all unique identities, complexities, and complications. I challenge readers to not let these stories remain on these pages. May the stories of Tyler, Eric, Donald, Rebecca, He Joonie, Valerie, Mark, Austin, and Jenna remain a part of you as you support youth coming from diverse backgrounds; support them, celebrate them, and be the one who inspires them to change their generation.

RESOURCES: FOR STUDENTS

Through the many stories shared from students making sense of their religion and sexuality, many resources were discussed. A brief overview of resources for students are listed below.

Becoming active in an LGBTQ Group: Many students sought out high school Gay Straight Alliance groups and found support and normalized their experiences. Students can find more information on developing a GSA from the GSA Network at www.gsanetwork.org

LGBT focused counseling: Many communities and campuses have counselors who specialize in gender and sexual identity. These can often be found by seeking advice from an LGBT center on campus or in a community.

Media: Positive portrayals of LGBTQ people in movies, magazines, books, and telelvision normalized the experiences students were having and allowed them to have a more positive self-percetion. Some examples include *Logo* TV, *Here* TV, *The Advocate* magazine, and *Out* Magazine.

Documentaries: There were many documentaries that students viewed to assist them with understanding their identiy, but two that were mentioned often were *For the Bible Tells Me So* and *Fish Out of Water.*

Literature: Many students facing challenges were majoring in Sociology or Feminist studies,which exposed them to writings from differen perspectives and tought them critical thinking skills. Informationa bout LGBTQ books can be found at www.lambdaliterary.org or find more book from Purble Books Publishing at www.purplebookspublishing.com.

Openly Affirming Churches: Many students needed a place that supported them spiritually and accepted their sexual idenity.
Wellness: Many of the students who shared their challenges faced extreme stress and anxiety. In order to remain emotionally stable they found ways to manage stress. Some of these methods included painting, excercising, playing music, journaling, or meditation.

Online Support: Many students faced intense emotional anguish and needed immediate counseling. In those situations students can find support at online resources, such as the Trevor Project at www.thetrevorproject.org and www.lambda.org/youth.htm.

Resources: For Educators

Students often spend more time with educator than with their families, so it is crucial they be prepared to assist studens while in need. A few reources to assist educators are listed below.

On-going Education: The issues related to LGBTQ youth constantly evolves, so it is crucial to stay updated on issues and how to best support. This can happen through attending a LGBTQ Ally training. Additional resources about supporting youth of color and transgender youth can be found at www.safeschoolscoalition.org.

Online Resources: There are many online resources designated for educators, such as The National Gay and Lesbian Task Force at www.thetaskforce.org and the Gay, Lesbian and Straight Education Netork (GLSEN) at www.glsen.org

Documentaries: Documentaries make on-going education more accessible. A basic documentary many educators can learn from is *Put This on the Map* found at www.putthisonthemap.org.

Policies: As educators it is crucial to understand insitutional policies and how to respond if hate or bias incidents occur. Forming a task force focused on LGBTQ issues could make this easier.

Mentorship: Openly LGBTQ-identifed educators were positive examples to students, and they could see role models who broke negative stereotypes.

Organizational resources: Students often talked to a faculty or staff member before talking to the campus LGBTQ professional or counselor. All campus educators must be aware of the resources on a campus or in a community, such as identity support offices, couneling services, and hate crime reporting systems.

RESOURCES: PARENTS

Parents and family members can often be the greatest supporter, but at times they can also be the greatest cause of conflict. Nearly all parents or family members aim to provide a loving and supportive environment for their student, and below are some brief resources.

On-going Education: Many parents aimed to be helpful, but often did not have the proper understanding or resources to assist their students. Parents should seek current information about LGBTQ identities, challenges, and ways to support. Gender Spectrum is an organization that provides education and training to parents about gender, mental health, and social servies; more inforation can be found at www.genderspectrum.org.

PFLAG: Parents, Families, & Friends of Lesbians and Gays (PLAG) is an organization with local chapteres that provides resources, support, and group meetings for parents of LGBTQ people. To find a local chapter once can visit www.pflag.org

Listening: Even if a parent is unsure who to respond, simply using active listening skills are geratly beneficial.

Online support: At times parents also need support and guidance. Families Matter provides safe, supportive, and confidential resources for parents of LGBTQ students and are available at www.familiesmatterusa.org.

Community resources: Parents should become familiary with community and campus resources. Many campuses and communities haves identity support offices, couneling services, and hate crime reporting systems.

Documentaries: Parents often are trying to make sense of the morality of their student's same-sex relationship and two documentaries can provide additional insights; *For the Bible Tells Me So* and *Fish Out of Water*.

REFERENCES

Astin, A. W. (1984). Student involvement: A developmental theory for higher education. *Journal of College Student Personnel*, 25, 297-308.

Barret, R. & Barzan, R. (1996). Spiritual experiences of gay men and lesbians. *Counseling & Values*, 41(1), 4-12.

Bess, H.H. (1995). Homosexuality in the evangelical experience. Open Hands, 11(3). Retrieved from http://www.clgs.org/homosexuality-evangelical-experience-0.

Buchanan, M., Dzelme, K., Harris, D., & Hecker, L. (2003). Challenge of being simultaneously gay or lesbian and spiritual and/or religious: A narrative perspective. *American Journal of Therapy*, 29(5), 435-449.

Burke, R.A., & Stabb, S.D. (1995). Gay, lesbian, and bisexual student needs. In S.D. Stabb & J.E. Talley (Eds.), *Multicultural needs assessment for college and university student population* (pp. 173-201). Springfield, IL: Thomas.

Cass, V.C. (1979). Homosexual identity formation: A theoretical model. *Journal of Homosexuality*, 4(3), 219-235.

Chickering, A.W., & Reisser, L. (1993). *Education and identity* (2nd ed.) San Francisco: Jossey-Bass.

Cohen, K.M., & Savin-Williams, R.C. (1996). Developmental perspectives on coming out to self and others. In R.C. Savin-Williams & K.M. Cohen (Eds.), *The lives of lesbian, gays, and bisexuals: Children to adults* (pp. 113-151). Fort Worth, TX: Harcourt Brace.

D'Augelli, A.R. (1992). Lesbian and gay male undergraduates' experiences of harassment and fear on campus. *Journal of Interpersonal Violence*, 7, 383-395.

D'Augelli, A.R. (1994). Identity development and sexual orientation: Toward a model lesbian, gay, and bisexual development. In E.G. Trickett, R.J. Watts, & D. Birman (Eds.), *Human diversity: Perspectives on people in context* (pp. 312-333). San Francisco: Jossey-Bass.

Griffin, H.L. (2006). *Their own receive them not: African American lesbians and gays in black churches.* Cleveland: The Pilgrim Press.

Hubbard, J. (2010, October 3). Fifth gay teen suicide in three weeks sparks debate. *ABC News.* Retrieved from http://abcnews.go.com/US/gay-teen-suicide-sparks-debate/story?id=11788128

Jeffries, W.L., Dodge, B., & Sandfort, T.G.M. (2008). Religion and spirituality among bisexual Black men in the USA. *Cult Health Sex*, 10(5), 463-477.

Kinnaman, D., & Lyons, G. (2007). *Unchristian: What a new generation really thinks about Christianity...and why it matters.* Grand Rapids, MI: BakerBooks.

Kraig, B. (1998). Faculty and staff mentors for LGBT students: Key responsibilities and requirement. In R. L. Sanlo (Ed.), *Working with lesbian, gay, bisexual, and transgender college students: A handbook for faculty and administrators*, (pp. 245-254). Westport, CT: Greenwood Press.

Levine, H., & Love, P.G. (2000). Religiously affiliated institution and sexual orientation. In V.A. Wall and N.J. Evans (Eds.), *Toward acceptance: Sexual orientation issues on campus* (pp. 89-105). Alexandria, VA: American College Personnel Association.

Moore, G. (2003). *A question of truth: Christianity and homosexuality*. New York: Continuum.

Poynter, K.J., & Washington, J. (2005). Multiple identities: Creating community on campus for LGBT students. *New Directions for Student Services,* 2005(111), 41-47.

Rankin, S. (2003). *Campus climate for gay, lesbian, bisexual and transgender people: A national perspective*. New York: National Gay and Lesbian Task Force Policy Institute.

Rankin, S, Weber, G, Blumenfeld, W, & Frazer, S. (2010). *2010 State of higher education: For lesbian, gay, bisexual & transgender people.* Charlotte, NC: Campus Pride.

Ritter, K.Y., & O'Neill, C.W. (1989). Moving through loss: The spiritual journey of gay men and lesbian women. *Journal of Counseling & Development*, 68, 9-15.

Rosser, B.S. (1991). Christian and Catholic background and adherence in New Zealand homosexually active males: A psychological investigation. *Journal of Psychology & Human Sexuality*, 3, 89-115.

Rosser, B.R.S. (1992). *Gay Catholics Down Under: The journeys in sexuality and spirituality of gay men in Australia and New Zealand*. Westport: Praeger Publishers.

Savin-Williams, R.C., & Cohen, K.M. (1996). *The lives of lesbian, gays, and bisexuals: Children to adults*. Fort Worth, TX: Harcourt Brace College Publishers.

Schuck, K.D., & Liddle, B.J. (2001). Religious conflicts experienced by lesbian, gay, and bisexual individuals. *Journal of Gay & Lesbian Psychotherapy*, 5, 63-83.

Scott, D. (1991). Working with gay and lesbian student organizations. In N.J. Evans & V.A. Walls (Eds.), *Beyond tolerance: Gay, lesbians, and bisexuals on campus* (pp. 117-130) Alexandria, VA: American College Personnel Association.

Sherry, A., Adlman, A., Whilde, M.R., & Quick, D. (2010). Competing selves: Negotiating the intersection of spiritual and sexual identities. *Professional Psychology: Research and Practice, 2*, 112-119.

Seow, C.L. (1996). *Homosexuality and Christian community*. Louisville, KY: Westminster John Knox Press.

Swanson, D.J. (2004, August). Neither cold nor hot: An analysis of Christian world web sites that address LGBT publics. Paper presented at the annual meeting of t he Association for Education in Journalism & Mass Communications, Toronto, Ontario, Canada.

Tigert, L.M. (1996*). Coming out while staying in: Struggles and celebrations of lesbian, gays, and bisexuals in the church*. Cleveland: United Church Press.

Wilcox, M. M. (2003). *Coming out in Christianity: Religion, identity, and community*. Bloomington: Indiana University Press.

Windmeyer, S.L. (2006). *The advocate college guide for LGBT students*. New York: Alyson Books.

Yip, A.K.T. (1996). Gay Christians and their participation in the gay subculture. *Deviant Behavior: An Interdisciplinary Journal, 17,* 297-318.

Yip, A.K.T. (1997). Attacking the attacker: Gay Christians talk back. *The British Journal of Sociology, 48* (1), 113-127.

APPENDIX A: INTERVIEW GUIDE

Opening: Informed consent, introductions, purpose of the study, small icebreaker questions

Screening Questions:

Are you a Christian?

Are you or have you been in a same-sex dating-relationship?

Topic Questions :

- Tell me about your family's religious background?
- How did you decide you were a Christian?
- How do you define "dating?" How do you define a "relationship?"
- Tell me about your early experiences being attracted to the same-sex?
- Can you tell me about your first relationship with someone of the same-sex? What was your partner's religious background?
- When you first began your relationship what were some feelings you had?
- How would you describe the ending of your relationship, if it has ended?
- What were some things you were feeling at the end of your relationship? If you were feeling some distress, how did you resolve it? What grounded you? If not feeling distressed, why? What grounded you?
- During the relationship how would you describe your religious life?
- Can you tell me more about your dating and relationship history during your time in college?

- Describe what you think God feels about your same-sex
- relationship(s)?
- Tell me about your participation with religious
- organizations, such as a Church, student ministry, Bible study, etc. Does your religious organization know you are/were in a same-sex relationship? What has been their response once they knew about your same-sex relationship? What are your feelings on their response?
- Does your family know you are/were in a same-sex relationship? What has been their response once they knew about your same-sex relationship?
- Describe how your religious life and your sexuality affect each other?
- If conflict was present, what do you think were the causes of the conflict between your Christianity and your same-sex relationship(s)?
- Describe how this conflict has affected you?
- Who did you turned to for help to resolve the conflict? Why? Were they religious?
- What has been helpful as you faced challenges related to your sexuality and religious life?

APPENDIX B: TABLE OF PARTICIPANTS' BACKGROUNDS

Table 1

Summary of Participants

Name	Religious Background	Sexual Identity	Race/Ethnicity	Institution Background
Austin	Pentecostal Christian, but exploring	Gay identified	White-American	Private Christian college and then public university both in the Midv
Donald	Protestant Christian	Gay identified	Multiracial	Private Christian college; Souther California
Eric	Pentecostal Christian and Catholic	Gay identified	Latino	Private Christian college and then separate public university; All i Southern Califo
He Joonie	Protestant Christian	Queer identified	Korean-American	Public university Southern Califo
Jenna	Catholic	Lesbian identified	White-American	Liberal arts coll Southern Califo
Mark	Baptist	Gay identified	Multiracial; African-American and White-American	Public university Midwest
Rebecca	Catholic	Bisexual identified	Multiracial; Latina and White-American	Liberal arts coll Southern Califo
Tyler	Protestant Christian	Gay identified	Black-American	Public university Midwest
Valerie	Catholic	Queer identified	Multiracial: Latina	Public university Southern Califo

APPENDIX C: CONSENT FORM

I agree to participate in the research project titled *Balancing Christianity and same-sex relationships: students finding peace with sexuality and spirituality* being conducted by Dr. Lemuel Watson and Joshua Johnson, a College of Education faculty member Counseling, Adult and Higher Education graduate student at Northern Illinois University. I have been informed that the purpose of the study is to understand how students balance a Christian life and a same-sex romantic relationship. Through exploring the experiences of these students we hope to better understand what were common struggles, experiences, and resources that have provided peace.

I understand that if I agree to participate in this study, I will be asked to do the following: participate in a group discussion by answering a variety of questions related to your personal experiences and feelings for approximately one hour.

I am aware that my participation is voluntary and may be withdrawn at any time without penalty or prejudice, and that if I have any additional questions concerning this study, I may contact Dr. Lemuel Watson at (815) 753-9055. I understand that if I wish further information regarding my rights as a research subject, I may contact the Office of Research Compliance at Northern Illinois University at (815) 753-8524.

I understand that the intended benefits of this study include hearing other students' struggles with common issues, hearing and understand what resources helped other students find peace with struggles, an opportunity to verbalize and explain experiences and emotions, and an opportunity to hear about campus and community resources.

I have been informed that potential risks and/or discomforts I could experience during this study include a) describing challenging life experiences, and b) participants may break confidentiality and share information about other participants. I understand that all information gathered during this experiment will be kept confidential by only using first names, not sharing any students' names or specific information which would disclose a students' identity, and notes and tape recordings will only be handled by the researchers and transcribers); however, I also understand that, when participating in a focus group, confidentiality among the members of the group cannot be guaranteed.

I realize that Northern Illinois policy does not provide for compensation for, nor does the University carry insurance to cover injury or illness incurred as a result of participation in University sponsored research projects

I understand that my consent to participate in this project does not constitute a waiver of any legal rights or redress I might have as a result of my participation, and I acknowledge that I have received a copy of this consent form.

_____

Signature of Subject   Date

I agree that a tape recorder may be used to record my voice and statements during this focus group or interview.

_____

Signature of Subject   Date

ABOUT THE AUTHOR

Dr. Joshua Moon Johnson is the Director of the Resource Center for Sexual & Gender Diversity/Lesbian, Gay, Bisexual, and Transgender Services and Women's Center programs at the University of California, Santa Barbara. Prior to joining UCSB, Dr. Johnson served as an Assistant Director in Housing & Dining and Residential Communities and Marketing and Public Relations at Northern Illinois University in addition to serving as the Acting Director of the Lesbian, Gay, Bisexual, Transgender Resource Center. While at NIU, Johnson also served as a teaching assistant for a Multicultural Education graduate seminar Prior to joining NIU, Johnson worked in residence life at Binghamton University, State University of New York. Dr. Johnson received a doctorate in higher education and a certificate in LGBT studies from Northern Illinois University, and his dissertation topic was on the experiences of Christian college students in same-sex relationships. Dr. Johnson received a master's degree in social sciences, student affairs, and diversity from Binghamton University, State University of New York, and his thesis was on university services for transgender students. Dr. Johnson also has a master's degree in marketing analysis from The University of Alabama as well as a bachelor's in business from the University of South Alabama.

Dr. Johnson has conducted research in South Korea and the Philippines on social justice and service learning in Asian higher education. Dr. Johnson was a visiting scholar at Sophia University in Tokyo, Japan at the Institute for Comparative Culture where he was conducting research on queer spaces in Tokyo. Dr. Johnson is an alumnus of the Social Justice Training Institute and has presented regionally, nationally, and internationally on topics such as media and marginality, queer people of color, multiracial student identity, intersections of religion and sexuality, and facilitating dialogues on diversity. Dr.

Johnson has numerous publications on topics such as multiracial student support and queer Asian Pacific Islander men as leaders in higher education. He is currently finishing a co-edited volume about LGBTQ leaders in higher education. Dr. Johnson is a trained diversity facilitator and serves as the National Association of Student Personnel Administrators (NASPA) Asian Pacific Islander Concerns Knowledge Community Representative for Southern California and previously for NASPA region IV. Dr. Johnson is also the co-chair elect for the MultiRacial Knowledge Community. Dr. Johnson is an instructor of Popular Culture and Identity and Communications at Brooks Institute of Art in Santa Barbara, California. He also hosts a weekly public affairs radio talk show on 91.9 FM, KCSB Santa Barbara called *Check Ya'Self*, which critically examines media and popular culture through a social justice lens. Much of Dr. Johnson's work stems from his personal identity as a queer, Christian, multiracial Asian-American/Euro-American, man who grew up in Mississippi, and was raised by Pentecostal ministers.